LEO P. ROCK, S.J.

MAKING FRIENDS WITH YOURSELF

Christian Growth and Self-Acceptance

 St Paul Publications

St Paul Publications
Middlegreen, Slough SL3 6BT, England

Copyright © 1990 by Leo Rock

First published in 1990 by Paulist Press, 997 Macarthur Boulevard, Mahwah, NY 07430

Cover: photo by Transworld Press
Printed by Guernsey Press Company Ltd, Guernsey C.I.
ISBN 085439 333 1

St Paul Publications is an activity of the priests and brothers of the Society of St Paul who proclaim the Gospel through the media of social communication

MAKING FRIENDS WITH YOURSELF

Contents

Foreword

In 1963 I was a second year Jesuit novice in the California province. It was fall of that year that I caught my first glimpse of Leo Rock. I remember having heard all sorts of stories about the man from people who knew him. I anticipated seeing, from all the reports, someone the size of Goliath. The reality was more like a young David. Small in physical stature but large in heart, as I was gradually to discover, I will never forget his vacuum cleaner eyes that seemed to take in everything and everyone in that room.

The philosopher Lao Tzu said that "a journey of three thousand miles is begun with one step." While I did not know this at the time, that evening was my first step on the road to "making friends" with Leo Rock.

In 1971 Leo Rock was asked by the California province to become director of novices. He felt ill-equipped for such a position. His background was clinical psychology. He felt more comfortable in that arena than in St. Teresa of Avila's *Interior Castle*. He felt himself more confidently equipped for the role of counselor than spiritual director. He soon "made friends" with his new job. Formation and the California province have never been the same.

In 1973 Leo asked a newly ordained Jesuit, who would later write the foreword to his first book, if he would come down and be his assistant. This young man was neither a clinical psychologist nor a spiritual director, but he did come from good peasant Irish stock. When I asked Leo what the job would entail, in order to gauge my aptitude for the position, he simply said: "Mike, I would like you to come down and do whatever you want to do. Your presence is what you will bring . . . to whatever you eventually do." This was disconcerting for someone who wanted clarity of job description. I was not at all sure I had what it took to be assistant director of novices. From 1973 to 1976 I learned the meaning of "making friends with good enough."

Over the years Leo has continued to be there when I needed a receptive ear, an understanding heart, a sign of hope, the positive challenge I did not want to hear, a word of wisdom, and, most importantly, a friend. I will, to my dying day, remember those healing words Leo Rock wrote about me during an experience which I considered the nadir of my life. In typically brief and succinct Rockonian rhetoric he simply stated: "Michael Moynahan is my friend." This was one of the most powerful experiences of grace that I have had in my life.

Leo Rock has been midwife to more people's imaginations, creativity and dreams than I care to count. Those who have been touched, encouraged, assisted in their healing process by his gentle, caring presence are legion. He is one of the best kept secrets of the California province. And now, through *Making Friends with Yourself*, the secret is out!

In the gospels we hear people describe Jesus as "speaking with authority, not like their own teachers." Readers beware. To read the pages that follow is to experience someone who speaks and writes with authority. That authority, that power, comes from the human honesty and truth that Leo Rock speaks. He speaks of what he knows. He shares with you some of his paschal experience, vision and wisdom. And in each page, each chapter, you will hear the ring of truth. If you let that truth in, if you learn how to "make friends" with that truth, it will transform you and ultimately set you free.

Michael E. Moynahan, S.J.

Author's Preface

It would have been grammatically more honest to have written this book in the first person singular. The reflections are mine; they grew out of my own experience and what the shared experience of others has taught me. I am the source of several of the anonymous quotes and anecdotes. Whatever biases, blind spots, or cases of plain foolishness send clouds scudding across the sky, these are all mine as well. My intention was not to deny or hide any of this, but to spare myself (and the reader) all those "I's."

But there was more to it than that. The temptation for all of us is to think that our private inner experience sets us apart from everyone else, marks us with the sign of Cain that only we can see, that our private experience of ourselves is somehow nuttier, more outrageous, more irrational than that of all those cool and composed others who surround us. So much do our public faces succeed in deceiving each other! It is true that, unshared, our private experience does set us apart from everyone else. Only when we have the courage to risk sharing it do we discover that what we think is true only of *me* is true of us. The "we" of the text, I hope, will remind the reader of this. And this, too: as Christians, each of us is called to be part of a *we;* an *I,* alone, is not enough, if we would be Christian.

I know nothing that I have not been taught by others: those wo have loved and cared for me, family and friends; teachers in the formal sense; those who have come to me for guidance and help and who have, by sharing themselves, helped and taught me more than they will ever suspect; my brother Jesuits. Whatever is of worth or value in this book is theirs as much as it is mine.

With special gratitude to the best of teachers, I dedicate this book to Kenney.

1. Making Friends with Introductions

*"I have come that they may have life and have it
to the full" (Jn 10:10).*

Picture a pond lying there on a windless day. The
surface is still. Toss pebbles, one by one, into the center of
the pond and each pebble sets in motion a ripple that
moves out in ever-widening circles till each gently nudges
the edges of the pond.

This is a pebble-tossing book, with the reader's mind
and heart the intended targets. There are no large stones
in this book, much less boulders. There is really nothing
even new in it. Pebbles are as common as horseflies and
brown grass in summer. The pebbles are relatively unimportant. It's those ripples on the surface of the pond that
pebble-tossing is all about.

We fall with insidious ease into the habit of telling
ourselves it's what others think that is important, rele-
gating our own thoughts to that back shelf where we keep
the stuff we should really throw away but don't have the
heart to—our junk. It's no accident that we do this. We
are taught from our earliest years to defer to our betters.
Others know better than we do. Children (up to and including the age of ninety-two) should be seen and not
heard. What do *we* know about it, anyway? Thus we learn
to confer on our thoughts, our opinions, our hard-won
experience a kind of second-class citizenship in a world of
brighter, more informed, more gifted others. And so we
tell ourselves what's important about reading a book is to
find out what the *author* thinks, how the *author* feels
about this, that, and the other, to benefit from the *au-*

thor's insights. Of course we tell ourselves this. This is what we've been trained to do.

In spite of all our training, the simple, undeniable fact is that *our* thoughts on the matter are all that count *for us. Our* thoughts determine our attitudes, our values, our hopes and dreams. Within the privacy of our inner selves no one's thoughts but *ours* hold sway, no one's experience but *ours* is constant companion to our conscious awareness. On one only subject each of us has been assigned the task of becoming the world's ranking expert: being *this* self which each of us is called to be. And this is one task that cannot be delegated to anyone else. Certainly we can learn from the thoughts and experience of others, but only to the extent that these help us discover what *we* think do these illuminate *our own* experience. Which brings us back to pebbles and ripples on ponds. And this book.

If this book has any value (after all, pebbles are only pebbles) it lies in this, that the thoughts expressed herein set in motion ripples in the minds and hearts of the readers. Whether the readers say "Yes, that's just how it is for me" or "That's not how I see it, that's not my experience" is unimportant. What *is* important is that the readers recognize more clearly and possess more respectfully their own thoughts and experience, that the readers take off from that back shelf their own thoughts on the matter. If this book succeeds in doing that, it has served its purpose.

Jesus Christ was the greatest pebble-tosser of all time. His pebbles, as all pebbles do, came from the ordinary, the commonplace, the familiar—and therefore the timeless. He picked them up wherever he found them: in a wheat field, among a flock of sheep, from children playing in a village square. Jesus knew it was not the pebbles that were important, but those ripples in the mind and heart. We call his word "the living word" precisely because his word has a unique power to set those ripples in motion.

The eternal question Jesus puts to us is: Who do *you* say I am? What do *you* think? Do *you* believe? Here, even God's own word defers to what *we* think.

We miss the whole point if we think divinity needed to enter into and put on our common humanity in order to understand it from the inside out, as if the incarnation were a divine exercise in self-education, a kind of field trip. God, the creator of all, is the source of all being. All that is images God's fullness of being. Not even all that is created, in its profligate variety and extravagant profusion, exhausts the imageability of God. God, as creator, is in all that is and knows it inside out. No, the point of the incarnation was not that *God* understand our humanity, but that *we* come to understand it. Yes, Jesus came to reveal to us who he is and who the Father is, but he did this in the only way possible: by showing us who *we* are, by telling us things about ourselves we had no other way of knowing, no other way of even suspecting. Which of us could have ever suspected that the creator of all that is not only loves us beyond reason but *likes* us as well? Which of us could have ever suspected that God's Holy Spirit lives within our skin and is closer to us, more vitally involved with us, than our own heartbeat? Who would *dare* think such presumptuous thoughts as these and others had not Jesus told us? Which is why Jesus' question to us always is: What do *you* think? And why he keeps tossing all those pebbles.

If our faith can be likened to a lamp, the only lamp given us to light the house we dwell in, do we not do this with it? We set it in the front room where we receive guests. While it quite nicely lights that room where we set it, the other rooms in our house are pretty much in darkness and shadows, depending on how much light they can catch from the windows, which at night isn't very much. We stumble around in the rooms where we actively live, saving the light for that front, guest-receiving room.

We do this with our faith without even realizing it.

Given us to shed light on *all* of our living, *all* of our experience, our faith is set off in its own corner: our God-corner,
our religion-corner. There is, on the one hand, our faith
and holy things—the things of God, and, on the other, the
decidedly unholy business of making a living and somehow dealing with the messy, outrageous, maddening, sinful realities we find both within ourselves and in that
larger world we inhabit. After all, everything has its
proper place, and everything in its place. Is not the very
reason we build cathedrals and churches, temples and
synagogues that God might be given a proper place? Are
not Sundays (or Saturdays) set off from the rest of the
week so that God might have a proper time?

What may make eminent good sense to our neat and
orderly minds and our passion to have everything in its
place has one small hitch. This is decidedly not the way
God sees things. God, not having read all our books and
therefore knowing no better, persists in being everywhere
and into everything, as befits the creator of all. The Holy
Spirit breathes everywhere, in season and out. Monday
belongs to God no less than Sunday. Main Street belongs
to God no less than the mountaintop. God roams through
all the rooms of our house, even the messiest, most clut-
tered. How often do we sit dressed in our company clothes
in the front room, waiting to receive God into our house,
while all the time God is already there in the den, the
kitchen, the bedroom? Then we complain that God didn't
come to see us.

If we are to give God and our faith their rightful place
in our lives, we have to learn to find God everywhere God
is, not just in those places we have set aside for God; we
have to learn to find God whenever God is, not just those
times we set aside for God. God attends to us everywhere,
if we could but see this. In every corner of our human
experience, even the darkest and most hidden corners,
God waits to be recognized. God attends to us all the time,
if we could but see this. Happy times, painful times; busy

times, quiet times; morning, noon, and night—God is there waiting to be recognized.

Faith is essentially a matter of facing in the right direction. Among all the wonderful faculties God has given us, eyes on the back of our heads are not included. We can see only in the direction we're facing. So much of what we don't see is simply a matter of facing in the wrong direction, like the neophyte traveler from California on the east coast for the first time who stood on the beach at sunset waiting for the sun to sink over the water as he'd known it to do all his California life. When we turn our back on what *we* think and face only toward what others think, we're facing in the wrong direction. When we turn our back on what *we* experience and face only toward what others experience, we're facing in the wrong direction. The Lord has his work cut out for him, getting us to turn around and face in the right direction.

It is by reflecting in faith on our human experience, readily available to us, that we learn to hear and recognize the voice of God's Holy Spirit speaking within, speaking *to us*. This book invites its readers to do just that. To let our faith bring light to *all* the rooms in our house, even the least lovely. To let our inner experience say to us all that it has to say to us, all that God has to say to us in it. We need not search far and wide to find God. God finds us; we don't find God. And, having found us, God waits within for our recognition, our welcome, our love. God's patience is beyond belief! But, then, God is used to being kept waiting, even being ignored. Fortunately for us, God does not take offense easily—not half as easily as we do, in fact.

Perhaps someday science will discover a way to isolate a smile from the face smiling, invent a one-sided coin, separate the sun from its light. Perhaps, someday; but don't bet on it. Some things are so inseparable you can't have one without the other. The very notion is ridiculous, is it not? Let us pause and consider this no small mystery.

Why is it, then, that we go to such lengths, contrive such strategems, choose such paths so as to separate ourselves from God, have ourselves without God? We do, of course. Not entirely without God, perhaps. But with as much of God as God wants to give us? Not if Jesus is to be believed. Is it that we want God, but just enough of God so as not to interfere with our plans or get in the way of our having fun? Or is it that we fear, as Francis Thompson put it in *The Hound of Heaven,* lest having him we have naught else besides? Is it that God's reputation is so bad we want as little as possible to do with God? There *have* to be reasons. How explain this curiously one-sided love affair that has been going on between God and us since it all began?

We pile all the reasons together and call them sin. Which is to answer one mystery with another. To paraphrase Pogo: sin is *us.* We cannot look to our stars, the entrails of birds, bad companions or faulty advice to find the reasons. We have to look to ourselves. Who and what is this enemy within us so bent on sabotaging God's love? on sabotaging our love? What does he wear? What does she look like? The reflections in this book might help us recognize some of the guises of this enemy within each of us. Our enemy. God's enemy.

If this book can be said to propose any one thesis it is this: If we would be friends with others, among them God, we have to make friends with our inner selves; if we would be at peace with others and God, we have to be at peace with our inner selves. That's the deal. That's the way God set it up. The two are inseparable. Perhaps, after all, our relationship with God and others is not the place to begin, but rather our relationship with our inner selves.

Jesus said this: "If you bring your gift to the altar, and there recall that your brother has anything against you, leave your gift there at the altar, go first to be reconciled with your brother, and then come and offer your gift" (Mt 5:23–24). If this is true for reconciliation between us and a brother or sister, how very much more true is it for reconciliation with our inner selves? If we would seek reconciliation with God and others, don't we first have to seek to be reconciled with ourselves? This book suggests some of the ways we can seek that reconciliation.

If we look at the wonders of unspoiled nature with the eyes of faith, we can see that everything there is just as God intended it to be. This funny, crooked cypress, that bird soaring in the sky, that mountain rising snow-capped in the distance, that surf crashing against the rocky coastline—*exactly* as God intended it! Whether we're consciously aware of it or not, this is why unspoiled nature leaves us awed, speechless, rapt: there we see an undistorted imaging of the creator. Nature believes in God. In all of nature we can find nothing that flees from what gives it life—except us. But is it God we are fleeing from or ourselves? Why do we flee from ourselves? What is it in us that we are fleeing from? These questions surely merit our careful attention, deserve the time we give to ponder our answers.

If, by some miracle, an oak tree were suddenly invested with our human faculties, would not something like this happen in short order? The tree, seeing itself mirrored in a pool of water, then seeing the other oaks, the pines, the plane trees growing around it, would say, "How did I go wrong? Why don't I have what they have? How have I displeased God that I should be like this?" It wouldn't take long for the oak tree to be filled with doubts (who am I?), self-blame (it's all my fault), hurt (nobody loves me), resentment (how can they treat me this way?), anger (I'll show them!). Finding little sympathy or comfort from without—those other trees, the sun, the soil, the water—the oak tree would eventually say, "I know! I'll be nothing but me. I'll have nothing to do with the other trees; they are not me. I'll have nothing to do with sun and air, water and soil; they are not me. I'll just be me." Then that oak tree would die. Let us thank God that oak trees and their ilk have been spared our human maladies.

While many physical maladies remain, as yet, heart-breakingly incurable, there are many for which we have found the cure. The process involves identifying the malady, isolating the malignant causes, and finding ways to neutralize their destructive action. Sinfulness in all its forms is a spiritual malady—perhaps better said, *the* spiritual malady, ultimately terminal. The temptation is to declare it incurable—at least for the majority of us who cannot afford the expensive and time-consuming cure—and go our merry way. The truth, as revealed by Jesus, is quite otherwise. There is a cure. Faith, hope, and love are cures. Openness to the indwelling Spirit of the Father and the Son is a cure. Openness to the goodness of our inner selves is a cure. The cure is, indeed, expensive, but not beyond our means. The cure does take time, but that's what time is for. This book suggests some of the symptoms of the malady and their causes, and some of the ways God has given us to neutralize their malignant action within us. Saints are living proof of the curability of the malady. For all of their immense differences from one another, saints have one thing in common: they let God love them, and so heal them.

Among the remedies suggested, be it noted, the acquisition of new intellectual insights is not high on the list. (Whether it is on the list at all is left to the discernment of the reader.) Most of us have enough intellectual insights to last ten lifetimes, with leftovers. What we so desperately need is not one more intellectual insight into truth, goodness, and love, but the *experience* of truth, goodness, and love, beginning with our own; not one more intellectual insight into the nature of God, but to *experience* God. Open minds are indispensable, but without open hearts, they just don't do it. Was it intellectual insight that led the Samaritan of Jesus' parable to delay his journey to help a down-and-out stranger? or that one leper to come back and say thank you to Jesus? or the first disciples to leave nets and counting house to follow Jesus? One rather doubts it.

It is easy for us to forget that our truth, as Christians, is primarily a person, not a collection of abstract assertions. Jesus Christ is our truth. Our response to our truth, for this reason, is not merely the kind of intellectual assent we bring to two-plus-two-equals-four. Full response to truth-as-person involves the heart as much as the head. It is primarily not, "I assent." It is, "I love." There's quite a difference.

Making friends is how the title of this book describes the contents. Making friends doesn't have all that much to do with acquiring intellectual insights, though it has a great deal to do with what is probably one of life's most rewarding *experiences*. Let us consider for a moment what we mean by the word "friend" when we use it discriminately. A friend, first and foremost, is someone we *like*. Yes, we love our friends, too, but, much more importantly, we *like* them. We do not like everyone we love. Parents, children, relatives, spouses, may also, if we are blessed, become our friends, but there is no divine law that guarantees this. Loving someone involves effort, often Herculean effort, sacrifice, large measures of pain, bewilderment, frustration. This is not to suggest the rewards are not well worth all these, only that the price is steep. Liking someone, by contrast, is almost ridiculously easy. There may be nothing fair about this, but that's the way it is.

We *enjoy* those we like. Every friendship has its serious moments, even its painful moments, but the prevailing climate is sunny and warm. Somehow we find ourselves laughing more with a friend, far more attuned to the ridiculous, the humorous, the playful. Perhaps that says it best: we can *play* together with friends. Working together is no measure of intimacy; we learn to work with all kinds of people. But those we choose to share our play, that is a different matter entirely. (In this context is it entirely whimsical to suggest that the Holy Spirit within us, far from the dour taskmaster we envision, is actually asking us to come out and play?)

Friends are a come-as-you-are experience. There is no need to dress up (though one may if one wishes), no need for party manners. One doesn't stand on ceremony with a friend. The rituals of friendship are made up as one goes along, easily discarded as new ones take their place; they are, after all, the rituals of relaxation and informality. Without any fuss, soul-searching, probing of each other's psyche, "meaningful" encounters, friends simply, well, *enjoy* each other's company. With a friend, as with true play, there is no *right* way to do anything, no self-conscious figuring out the correct move. Any spontaneous move is all right. Friends take each other just as they are, faults and all. Strangely, even faults can become as endearing in a friend as virtue. To suppose, for these reasons, that friendship such as this is shallow or does not involve our *real* selves is a serious misjudgment—the same misjudgment that says play is, by definition, shallow, trivial, not as self-involving as work is.

Why do friends like one another? One might just as well ask why one likes chocolate ice cream or baked potatoes. The reasons are beside the point. Friends can be just like us or so wildly different from us we wonder how on earth we can be friends. Friends may agree or disagree on any number of subjects—it makes no difference. Age, race, ancestry, religious persuasion, political affiliation —friendship laughs in the face of these. Perhaps that's because friendship knows how to laugh.

As with surprisingly so much else in our lives that is of rare value, we really don't *make* friends, as the expression has it; we allow them to *happen* to us. Friends happen to one another. The more we simply allow it to happen, the more friendship blooms; the more we try to take over, control and manage it, make all the right moves, the more we ruin it.

The essence of friendship is this: two people like one another enough simply to allow each other to be, instinctively welcoming and enjoying the other as is. Friends understand each other wordlessly—and laughingly.

Is it reading something into the story that wasn't there to see that Jesus *liked* Peter? Big, bluff, one-and-a-half-feet-in-his-mouth Peter. Mighty of temper (hacking off ears), mighty of heart Peter. Boastful, with his share of male vanity Peter. Shy and humble ("Lord, depart from me for I am a sinful man") Peter. The thought of anyone so much as harming a hair of his friend's head enraged Peter, yet, when the chips were down, Peter faltered, a coward. Is it seeing something that wasn't there to see Peter, arm thrown across his smaller friend's shoulders, laughing uproariously at his latest goof? How can one read the poignant account of their final encounter by that lake shore (given us by someone else who liked Peter?), when Jesus so compassionately elicited the triple profession of love that healed the triple denial, without seeing how much Jesus *liked* Peter?

So this book is about making friends, which is to say, it is about liking and enjoying, learning to understand, to laugh at, to let happen. Ourselves. Others. God. Perhaps even this book.

Stained-glass windows cannot be appreciated at night, even if we turn on every light in the cathedral. No matter what artistry went into their design and execution, what magnificent glass went into their construction, stained-glass windows come alive in all their splendor only when there is light coming *through* them. No amount of light shining *on* them can do the same. We are like stained-glass windows in this regard. To focus the light of our attention on ourselves may have us faced in the right direction to see ourselves, but only the light of the Holy Spirit shining *through* us allows us to see the artistry that went into our design, the magnificence of every piece of us, the beauty of us when God shines through us.

This, too, we do not have to (we cannot) make happen. We have only to allow it to happen. God does the rest.

You Are Road

You are road, mine the feet
That seek their uneasy way
Toward unknown destinations.

You are light, mine the eyes
That look so hungrily
For something, anything, everything.

You are word, mine the ears
That listen for an unheard sound
In the silent clamor of my heart's desiring.

And when we meet, Lord,
And if we meet, Lord,
Will I know it's You?

And when we meet, Lord,
And if we meet, Lord,
Will You be my way, my light, my word?

I dare to hope so,
Even as I fear so.

2. Making Friends with "I Don't Know"

"Father, forgive them for they know not what they do" (Lk 23:34).

> The solution to _____ (fill in the blank with the problem of your choice) is _____ (fill in the blank with the solution of your choice, in twenty-five words, or less.)

We are a nation of problem-solvers: identify the problem, find the solution. Everything from think-tanks to gurus, from editorial and advice columns in the newspapers to the slick promises of advertising besiege us with solutions to every problem under the sun. There is no dearth of experts willing, not to say eager, to fill in the above blanks for us. The confidence and conviction with which they propose their solutions is intimidating, defying the reservations of minds smaller than their own. How dare we amateurs doubt or question their expertise? Is not an expert, by definition, one who has the answers?

Were it not for the exceedingly inconvenient testimony of history, we could well answer yes, stifle our small-minded doubts and be done with it. But even the most benign reading of history reveals the remarkable frequency with which the experts have been wrong. Time has a most uncomfortable way of telling the truth. For, when it comes to problems and their solutions, there is a fairly clear-cut, unmistakable criterion for knowing a solution is the right one: the problem is solved, goes away, disappears, or, at the very least, is notably lessened. By this standard one hardly stands guilty of nit-picking if one experiences less than full confidence in many of the answers proposed by experts.

Unfortunately, given the state-of-the-art gloss of salesmanship and manipulating opinion, it is far too easy to forget history, too easy to dismiss one's doubts and questions as unworthy, too easy to fall prey to the delusion that we stand alone with our unanswered questions, surrounded by others who *do* know, who *do* have the answers. It is still tragically easy to convince ourselves that the emperor really is wearing his brand new clothes.

How many of us can find in the analogy of railroad tracks a way to describe something of our experience? There are two rails running parallel to each other. When one can see far enough down the tracks, the rails come closer and closer together and become one. Only if one travels far enough along the tracks does one realize that their coming together is an optical illusion. The rails are, indeed, parallel: they never meet and become one; they remain two.

Rail I is the rail on which everything is *said* about life: by parents, teachers, the books we read, what we hear from the pulpit, what we overhear others say as they talk about themselves and their lives, even many of the things we say to ourselves. Rail I tells us how life *is* or *should* be, how *we* should be. In fact, there are all kinds of shoulds and oughts on Rail I. There are also clear and distinct ideas about the very essence of all that is, insights into how everything works. On Rail I we can be caught up in the sheer luminous clarity of it all and exclaim, "Of course, how true! How very true!" If we were dealing with a monorail, everything would be fine at this point. But there's that second rail.

Rail II is the rail on which we *live* our lives. Rail II is where we *experience* ourselves and our lives. And, oh, the difference! Different from what all the books say with such clarity and conviction. Different from what everyone says about how everything *should* be, ourselves included. Nothing is really all that clear-cut on Rail II. Far from figuring ourselves out, understanding finally who we are and exactly what makes us tick, on Rail II we stubbornly remain largely a mystery to ourselves: unpredictable, full of not always pleasant surprises, capable of goodness in ways that leave us in awe of ourselves, no less capable of gross selfishness and evil that leave us ashamed of ourselves. Each time we think we've pinned ourselves down, tabbed and labeled ourselves, we find out once again that we aren't any *one* thing. Kind and sweet sometimes, yes, but incredibly thoughtless and cruel at other times. Intelligent and eminently reasonable at times, yes, but blind and stupid at others. We aren't any *one* thing. Many of us, too ashamed to confess how we really are to anyone else, can go on thinking that we are the only one on Rail II, that everyone else is over there on Rail I, that some grievous lack or sin has stranded us on Rail II while everyone else was crossing over to the other rail. And, because hope springs eternal, we can believe that, if we travel far enough down the tracks, the two rails will simply come together and become one, and we'll finally be where everyone else is.

It takes quite a bit of living, and the help of others who are willing to take the risk of sharing their own experience, to make the discovery that not only are we not alone on Rail II, but *everyone* lives on Rail II. The discovery can be the beginning of the end of isolation and alienation. It also takes quite a bit of living, of traveling down the tracks, to discover that the two rails never do meet and become one. *Understanding* life and *living* life are now and forevermore two distinctly different realities. Yes, intellectual understanding is an indispensable ingredient of human life, but even human life is first and foremost to be *lived*. As the old Irish proverb has it, you can't plow a field by turning it over in your mind. Life presents us with questions whose answers can be discovered only in the living out of our possibilities. May not many of our attempts to *understand* life be cleverly disguised escapes from the truly awesome responsibility of just *living* it? Attempts, really, somehow to cross over from Rail II, with all its exigencies, to Rail I?

One last consideration before we leave this analogy. Our temptation is to situate God and faith on Rail I. If we do, we mentally separate our real selves from God and faith. God is where we are, and that's on Rail II. Faith is given us to light our way, and that's on Rail II.

The more we manage to convince ourselves that we are surrounded on all sides by others who do have the answers, the more difficult it is for us to face our own not knowing without feeling stupid, inadequate, and inferior to the *cognoscenti*. After all, if *they* can know so clearly, what's wrong with us? If *they* have the answers, we ought to be able to find them as well.

None of us likes to feel stupid, inadequate, or inferior. In fact, these feelings are suffocating. We have at our disposal, however, the means to avoid these feelings: self-deception, in which each of us is truly expert and artist! If admitting to ourselves we really don't know is personally demeaning, we can spare ourselves this painful admission of our ignorance. The number of ways we have to do this is limited only by the inventiveness of our imaginations.

We can capitulate to the always-available-on-any-subject experts. Setting aside our misgivings, we can wholeheartedly, if mindlessly, adopt their answer as our own, no questions asked, give it our good name, a place in our home, raise it as our own. Or, again, if our answers persist in not adequately fitting our questions, we can artfully trim the questions to fit the answers, snipping off what doesn't fit, the way we trim a piece of cloth to fit its chosen place in the pattern. And the left-over scraps? We can always use them for patchwork quilts. Or, like the

inventive cook who substitutes one ingredient for another, more expensive, ingredient in a recipe, we can
always substitute comforting convictions for distressful
doubts. Given sufficient motivation, we can convince
ourselves with alarming ease. We are, God help us, end-
lessly inventive. And so, yes, we can convince ourselves
that we do know when we don't, or that we know more
than we actually do.

But why all the fuss? Where, after all, is the harm in a
bit of innocent self-deception to keep us warm on those
cold winter nights? Isn't there a place for Santa Claus and
the tooth fairy, for face-saving, for, shall we say, a certain
artistic license in dealing with the otherwise dreary facts
of life, if this is to be a kinder and gentler world and we,
kinder and gentler people? Tinted glasses do cut down the
glare. An edited text is easier to read. Rough edges can
cut, including the unvarnished truth's. All so seductively
reasonable. Everybody does it. What's the big problem?

The problem is this: self-deception, however comforting for the moment, is never innocent, which is to say,
harmless. We may ignore reality but that doesn't make it
go away. We may judiciously edit reality but that doesn't
change it. The longer we delay paying the due bills that
reality inexorably sends us, the more we owe. When it
comes to reality, there is no declaring bankruptcy and
having one's debts written off. Sooner or later self-deception always costs more than it saves.

Nowhere is this more true than in convincing ourselves we know when we don't know. The pathetic groups
of people who periodically show up, convinced beyond
doubt they know the day, if not the hour, that the world is
going to come to an end: they dispose of their worldly
goods and take themselves off to a mountaintop to await
Armageddon. When, by some miscalculation, the sun
rises on yet another day, they come down off the mountain and return to their calculations. The error, obviously,
is not in their calculations but in their unrecognized igno-

rance. We in fact have it on the best authority that we know neither the day nor the hour.

Less dramatically, but no less foolishly, we clutch our counterfeit convictions, pretending we know when we actually don't really know, pretending we have the answer when we have only a small piece of it. The price we pay for doing this is the mismanagement of ourselves, our lives, our world. The man who knows beyond a doubt that it is all his wife's fault—if only *she* would change all would be well with their marriage—is aimed with deadly precision toward a broken marriage. The woman who is totally convinced that career success is worth every sacrifice, including the sacrifice of relationships, values, self-respect, condemns herself to an increasingly empty and lonely existence. The hurts we inflict on one another, the misunderstandings, the false starts, the dead ends, our disappointments, our heartaches, our failures—so many of these are the price we pay for thinking we know when we don't.

When we convince ourselves that what we know is all there is to it, we close our minds to the element of *mystery* in all that is. We do this when we reduce ourselves or others to what we know, or think we know, about ourselves and others. We do this when we reduce God to what we know, or think we know, about God. The simple truth is there is more to us than we can ever know, more to life than we can ever know, infinitely more to God than we can ever know of God. Each time we have the courage and honesty to recognize and accept "I really don't know," we open our minds to the mystery of all that is, a richness so vastly more than anything our minds can contain.

Half a truth may be better than none, but only if we know it's only a piece of the truth, not the whole of it. Nothing closes the mind more effectively than the conviction one knows it all, has all the answers. Bigots and fanatics of every stripe suffer from minds that are irrevo-

cably closed against any possibility of their changing.
They have, indeed, made up their minds once and for all;
and in doing so, they have closed their minds. Isn't learning simply the process of *changing* our minds? How and
what we thought ten years ago is different from how and
what we think today; at least, it is if there has been any
learning going on in the meantime. Praying that does not
change our minds is dubious prayer. We can change our
minds only if we are willing to admit we don't yet know
it all.

As any devotee of spy thrillers and tales of espionage
knows, the point of the whole enterprise is (1) to keep
one's secrets safe from the enemy and (2) to ferret out the
enemy's secrets. One of the most effective weapons in the
arsenal of the trade has come to be known in the deplorable lexicon of that trade as "disinformation." Disinformation is information that is deliberately false (hence
safeguarding the real, but secret information), but still
close enough to the real information as convincingly to
mislead the enemy into thinking it *is* the real information.
Its whole purpose is to deceive. One classically successful
such deception involved the landing site of the invasion of
Europe which eventually brought World War II to an end.
The enemy *was* successfully disinformed, was misled into
thinking the invasion was coming somewhere else. Disinformation. It's worse than no information. That's why
it's such an effective weapon in the business of keeping
secrets.

Disinformation. As with radiation, exposure to it
above certain levels is hazardous to one's health. And yet,
are we not exposed to massive doses of disinformation
every day? Advertising, edited and slanted news, sales
pitches of every kind—these are only the more blatant
examples of disinformation as art form. As in so much
else, though, it is not so much what others do to us but
what we do to ourselves that is most damaging. Each time

we tell ourselves we know when we don't know, we deliver to ourselves another piece of disinformation, if skillfully enough done, close enough to the truth to pass for it, but basically false. Every time we do this we treat ourselves as the enemy. We may successfully keep the secret (I don't know) safe from the enemy. But that's simply stupid when the enemy is *us*.

Paradoxically, "I don't know" is an admission, not primarily of ignorance but of understanding. For the more we truly know and understand, the more aware we are of how little we know, of how much we don't yet understand. The more experienced we are, the less likely we are to be taken in by the facile, all-encompassing answers. A little knowledge *is* a dangerous thing, because the less we know, the easier it is to think we know it all, like the young man who was amazed at how much his *father* had learned from the son's eighteenth to twenty-first birthdays.

How many breakthroughs and discoveries have awaited the one who found the right question to ask? Only when we find the right question to ask is there any possibility of finding the right answer. Asking the right question aims us in the direction of the answer. Admitting "I don't know" is the first step on the way to asking the right questions.

We spend so much of our time asking ourselves the wrong questions. "What's in it for me?" instead of "What do I have to give to this situation?" "What do others think of me?" instead of "What do I think of myself?" "How can I find what I can love?" instead of "How can I love what I find?" "What will help me feel good?" instead of "What will help me be good?" The wrong questions are dead ends: they neither come from life nor lead to life.

Remember the story of the three blind men led to their first elephant? The one at the tail said, "An elephant is thin and round like a rope." The one at the trunk said,

"No, an elephant is thick and round like the trunk of a tree." The one at the side said, "You are both wrong: an elephant is flat like a wall." We grasp only parts of the truth, depending on our point of view, yet how often we talk ourselves into believing we grasp all of it. Convinced we have all of it, we see no need for further exploration, discussion, questioning.

Before we congratulate ourselves on our astuteness in grasping the point of the fable of the three blind men, and relish our superiority over them, let us remember our privileged position vis-à-vis the fable: unlike the blind men, we have *seen* an elephant in its entirety, in the flesh or at least in pictures. That's the only reason we can grasp the point so readily. But what about virtually every subject of debate, difference of opinion, rival-ism? What about all the rival claimants on truth? What about *our* claims on it? None of us has seen truth—on *any* subject —in its entirety. In this we are in the same situation as the blind men were. Which is the real point of the fable.

This matter of what we know and what we don't isn't merely some abstract nicety of philosophy, of concern only to those who happen to have an interest in epistemology. It affects the day-to-day quality of our human experience, our interactions with one another, and ultimately the life and breath of our faith. St. Paul described well that experience of at once knowing and not knowing which is at the core of faith: "Now we are seeing a dim reflection in a mirror . . ." (1 Cor 13:12). Unless we have courage and honesty enough to face squarely the limits of our knowing, our faith is diminished. If one knows everything, after all, what need is there for faith?

Faith carries us beyond the limits of what we can otherwise know, but faith says, "I believe," not "I understand." We climb to the top of the ridge so that from its top we can look out at the panorama that lies beyond the ridge on which we stand, a panorama not visible from below. Our climbing steps can be likened to our merely human categories of knowing: they bring us to the point from which we can see far beyond where our feet are planted. This seeing-beyond is what we call faith. We may not know or understand all that we see out there, but we can *see* it, nonetheless. Faith enables us to see what lies beyond our understanding, what lies beyond our human categories.

If we don't look carefully enough, we don't even notice how Jesus turned our human categories—the very foundations of our human judgments—topsy-turvy. First and last, the greatest and the least, strength and weakness, wisdom and foolishness, even, incredibly, life and death. The Son of the Father was trying to tell us, in yet another way, that the Father's categories and ours not only do not coincide, but more often than not are at odds with one another. Anyone who has ever tried to teach must surely have empathy for the all-but-impossible task laid on Jesus: to teach us to look beyond the narrow confines of our most cherished and honored human categories and see how much there is that is not contained by our categories.

When one sees with the eyes of faith, nothing is only what it seems to be. An infant wrapped in swaddling clothes. And, at the other end of that life, a man dying in shame and disgrace, a failure and an outcast from his God-centered society, leaving behind an inexplicably empty tomb. And a message of life and love and God that two thousand years, in spite of every ingenious method tried, have not silenced.

When one sees with the eyes of faith, nothing is only what it seems to be. All those supposedly accidental eventualities of our lives that have had us meet the people we met, been in those particular places at that particular time, turned this way rather than that. Fate? Luck? The seeming personal disasters that have turned us and our lives around into a richness unimagined before. Perhaps it is only in looking back, with the eyes of faith, that we can see that nothing is only what it seems.

The only true wisdom is to see as God sees, whose ways are as far above ours as the heavens are above the earth. We see only endings; God sees new beginnings— the seed falling into the ground to become plant and flower and fruit. Whether the ending is disappointment, failure, or even death itself, we see only the emptiness that haunts the dark hours of our nights; God sees our capacity to be filled with all that God has and wants to give us of light to fill our dark hours, of strength to fill our weakness, of love to fill the hollow places of our hearts. We see only what our unaided efforts can accomplish, which is never enough; God sees what can be accomplished by the mind open to God's truth and the heart open to God's love, which is everything. When one sees with the eyes of faith, one sees as God sees, which is why, when one sees with the eyes of faith, nothing is only what it seems. Not even ourselves.

Over and above all the common-sense reasons for doing so, it is faith, ultimately, that demands of us that we make friends with "I don't know." Faith, for one who has all the answers, is just so much excess baggage, the last resort of the fearful. For such, faith is a precarious proposition, at best, with too many ifs and far too many unknowns, whereas certainty is a sure bet—or so it seems. When we choose the path of faith we leave certainties behind and walk with unknowing. One need not be a mystic to know something about the cloud of unknowing. The results are often surprising.

The parents faced an awesomely difficult decision regarding their nine year old son: risk open-heart surgery (at a time when the risks were considerably greater than they are now) which, if successful, would allow their son to lead a normal life, or avoid the risk of surgery and let

their son continue to live as an invalid. They decided to
give their son a chance at a normal life. He died the day of
surgery. The priest who was the hospital chaplain, in answer to the emergency summons, arrived in pediatrics
just in time to hear the surgeon saying to the parents and
one set of grandparents, "We tried everything we could. It
just didn't work." Then the doctor turned and left. Then
the nurse was ushering the stunned family and the no
less stunned priest into a room, closing the door as she
left. The family sat, the shock written on their faces. The
priest sat, desperately asking himself, "What can I say?"
Everything that occurred to him sounded unforgivably
banal and empty. With growing desperation he realized
he *just didn't know* what to say. So he sat in silence,
feeling stupid, inadequate, a failure and a fraud. After
what seemed a lifetime to him, the father turned to the
mother and said, "Well, we'd better go and see about ar-
rangements." The family stood, still in shock, and left the
room. The priest cursed himself for a fool. The following
week he received a letter from the mother. She wrote, "As
long as I live I will be grateful to you for being there with
us in our grief. I cannot tell you what a help and consola-
tion to us your presence was." The priest had had the
courage to make friends with "I don't know." As it turned
out, his confused, painful silence (because it was genuine,
the truth?) had said more than any words he could have
devised.

Conventional wisdom, to say nothing of her family
and friends, clearly said that the right thing to do was to
proceed directly into graduate school after graduation.
After all, she had already been accepted by the school of
her choice. She had been over the pros and cons till her
mind grew fuzzy. Everything told her to get on with it.
And yet a nagging sense of "I just don't know" would not
leave her. Was now the right time? She faced it: she really
didn't know. So she deferred graduate school and applied
to a volunteer program in which she worked for two years,

in which she learned more about herself than any academic program could have taught her, in which she met and came to know her future husband. After two years she did proceed to graduate school, immensely grateful for all the two years had given her. She, too, had made friends with "I don't know."

As we retrace in memory the steps of our own life journey, can we not find the same? In retrospect, we can see it was not at all, as we sometimes think, a clearly planned itinerary, a carefully laid out route across an already mapped landscape, all reservations and accommodations made in advance by an obliging travel agent. No. If we see what was truly there, we see none of this. We see that our journey was actually through a *terra incognita,* a new and as-yet-unknown land. We see that, like the early explorers, we encountered ever new, unexplored territories—frontiers in ourselves, frontiers in our life. What lay beyond the frontier? Desert or fertile valley? More mountains to be crossed or level plains? Uninhabited land, friendly natives, a benign climate, water and food enough for the journey? We really didn't know until we had advanced and explored it. And as one frontier became known, familiar, settled, life called us on to the next. Life and growth call us to be explorers, not settlers, call us not to back away in fear from "I don't know" but to embrace it and let it carry us forward over the next horizon to what lies beyond. Always a new horizon until our journeying is, at last, done.

If it does nothing more than have us pause and reconsider before proceeding ahead, making friends with "I don't know" can set us free. Free to consider other options, other possibilities. Free to discover new truths, open unusual doors, explore beyond the frontiers of what we do know.

We should hardly be surprised. Jesus told us that the truth would set us free. Even when the truth is "I don't know."

Pentecost

Fire—that plays with light and shadow.
Fire—that warms, that burns.
Fire—that dances, jumps, delights the eye,
Consumes.
How apt an image, Lord, for the Spirit of You,
Breathing on us,
In us.

No wonder You are comfort,
Yet terror, too.
No wonder You enlighten
And confuse.
Our certainties melt
In the heat of Your fire,
Our cherished ways
Reduced to ash.

You promised, You prayed
—Oh, awful threat!—
That we'd be one
As You and Father are one.
See how Your Spirit burns away
Our differences! Language.
Race. The very walls
That shelter, shut us in our selves.
Annihilated. Made nothing
By Your Spirit's fiery breath.

So, breathless, we pray:
Come, Holy Spirit,
Blow us away!

3. Making Friends with Time

There is a season for everything, a time for every occupation under the heaven: a time for giving birth, a time for dying; a time for planting, a time for uprooting what has been planted. A time for killing, a time for healing; a time for knocking down, a time for building. A time for tears, a time for laughter; a time for mourning, a time for dancing. A time for throwing stones away, a time for gathering them up; a time for embracing, a time to refrain from embracing. A time for searching, a time for losing; a time for keeping, a time for throwing away. A time for tearing, a time for sewing; a time for keeping silent, a time for speaking. A time for loving, a time for hating; a time for war, a time for peace (Eccl 3:1–8).

Time is a dimension of our human experience that permeates everything we do, affects all we are. Like the air we breathe, as long as all goes well we pay it little attention and we take it for granted. Time gives us a past, a present, and a future. Time gives our life-story a beginning, a middle, and an ending, in small ways and large marking the chapters of our story. Time has much to do with our encountering God, with our journey in faith and hope and love. We do well to reflect on this all-pervasive dimension of our created reality, this inescapable ingredient of our human experience here on earth.

As we seem to do with most things that are at once simple and complex, we misperceive time in so many ways. And because we misperceive what time is all about, we set up an adversary relationship with time, evidenced in such expressions as "time is the enemy" and "fighting against time." As if time were an unwelcome intruder in an otherwise happy existence. We can think of time as if it were offered us on a take-it-or-leave-it basis, the way the hostess offers gravy for the mashed potatoes. If time and the demands of time don't appeal, then set them aside, ignore them, pretend they don't exist. To this way of thinking, time—like fatal accidents—is something that happens to other people. We can think of time as something that only takes away from us: takes away our youth, takes away our health, takes away our present—and gives nothing in return. Time, the rapacious thief. This list of indictments could go on, all of them due to the ways we misperceive time.

Think about the adverb "again." The human race, at some point in our collective past, recognized that the seasons of time are cyclic and that it would be a good thing to find a way to keep track of time. The seasons of the year return with enduring regularity: spring, summer, autumn, winter. Night follows day no less regularly. The way we keep track of time necessarily reflects this recurring cycle. Twenty-four hours in a day; seven days in a week; twelve months in a year. The method by which we keep track of time gives birth to the adverb "again." It is Monday again. It is autumn again. It is Christmas again. "Again" is the artificial by-product of the way we keep track of time. In truth, there is no such thing as again.

In real time nothing is ever again. It only seems that way. Today is not a replay of last Thursday, nor is it a preview of next Thursday. The simple truth is that today never happened before nor will it ever happen again. Today is a newly-minted coin that can be spent only once —today; it cannot be hoarded up for future contingencies.

A man took a vacation trip with a friend through the Canadian Rockies. On a wonderfully clear day they rode the aerial tram to the top of a mountain near Jasper. The view was breathtaking: the valley far below with its river winding its way through fields and forest, snow-covered mountains in the surrounding distance. The man said to himself: You will never be here again, so look carefully. He did, and etched indelibly on his memory that magnificent view.

Would we not look more carefully if we remembered that we pass this way only once, that there is no such thing as "again"? How heightened our awareness and sensitivities, how carefully we pay attention in those situations we know are for the last time: a loved one dying, leaving home, graduations, retirements—all the ways life bids us say farewell. And how heedlessly we can move through our days, scarcely noticing the opportunities each day offers. After all, we tell ourselves, we can always take care of it the next time around, when we come this way again. And so, "again" can insidiously become the delusion we use to justify our half-hearted response to what here-and-now asks of us, to what today offers us. We speak of once-in-a-lifetime opportunities. In the profoundest sense, is not every opportunity that life offers us once-in-a-lifetime? It indeed is if we pass this way one time only.

Thanks to memory, there is a place in our consciousness for our past. Thanks to our imagination, there is a place in our consciousness for our future. Our past and our future can certainly enrich our present, but they cannot *substitute* for it.

Precisely because there is no such thing as again, what is past is over and done with. There is not the slightest detail of yesterday we can change or undo today. We cannot rewrite the script, redirect yesterday's scene. The curtain has fallen on yesterday and that scene is finished. As long as clay is raw and soft we can shape and reshape it as many times as we want. Once the clay is fired, though, it is set; it's too late to reshape it. The past is like fired clay: set beyond the possibility of reshaping. This seems so obvious, doesn't it? And yet, how much time and energy we can steal from our present vainly trying to reshape our past! We can stew guiltily over past mistakes, past sins, past failures in ways that take our attention away from the present and what the present asks of us, from the redemption the present offers us. Or, conversely, we can try to recapture past innocence, past joys, past successes (always, of course, rendered larger and more rosy through the looking glass of memory), instead of attending to what today asks, what today offers.

One of the reasons the siren song of the past exercises such a strong attraction is the way in which we idolize youth. Billion dollar industries thrive on propagating the delusion that youth is the fleeting moment when the cup of life runneth over, when one's quota of happiness is virtually unlimited, the fullness of human existence. And afterward? The cup is inexorably drained, one's quota of happiness is steadily curtailed, life gradually falls away from its fullness. This carefully—and profitably—nurtured delusion says to us, in effect: if you are no longer young, at least have the grace to *seem* young—to dress young, to act young, to think young. As if aging were a shameful disgrace, all signs of which to be hidden, disguised, denied by the more than ample means at our disposal for just that purpose.

This cultural phenomenon doesn't even do justice to youth. Yes, youth is a time of boundless energy and large enthusiasms, when everything is possible, when the horizon stretches forever, when all there is is there for the asking. Or so it seems. Having small wisdom and even less experience, the young can enjoy the luxury of certitudes that are impervious to doubt or qualification. And yet, at the same time, youth is one of the most painful and confusing of times, a time when the sheer weight of unanswerable questions can be a crushing burden. Suicide among the young is a grim refutation of the unalloyed joys of youth propagated by the delusion. Most of us can be humbly grateful that we *survived* our youth.

This myth of golden youth sees time as only taking away. The truth is that every age of life offers unique gifts as well as unique challenges. If the body does, in fact, decline with age, this is more than offset by the opportunities for the expansion and growth of the spirit. As the excitement of the new wears off, the comfort of the familiar comes to take its place. When the level of activity and its satisfaction has to be curtailed, there is the opportunity to discover the deeper satisfactions of *being*. True friends, like good wine, only improve with age. The late afternoon sun has none of the brilliance of high noon, but it is a softer light, easier on the eyes, allowing shadows to highlight the shape of things not seen at noon. And without the night we could not see the stars.

Behind us is our past to lure us away from our present; ahead of us lies our future with the same potential to lure us away from our present. Our future lures us away from our present every time we try to live tomorrow today. We can, to a certain extent (but not nearly so much as we think), plan now for our future, but we cannot *live* it now. Worry is the price we pay for trying to live tomorrow today. It is not the here-and-now problem right in front of our face that causes worry. We're too busy dealing with the problem to have time to worry. Worry is the companion of all those what-ifs, might-be's, and even likely-will-be's of tomorrow—all those bridges we try to cross before getting to them, most of them never even materializing.

It is good and holy to remember our past. That's where we've come from. Our past has much to tell us and teach us. Like votive candles burning at a shrine, our memories light the sacred places in our hearts. So, too, it is good and holy to look to our future. That's where we're going. Our hopes and aspirations for the future give a depth and meaning to our present that would otherwise not be there. Yet, let it be said again, neither past nor future exempts us from our present and what our present asks of us. To allow either to rob us of the present—as we do in small ways and large—is to aid and abet in the crime of "killing time."

Every once in a while a phrase born of the vernacular expresses a truth far more profound than that intended. "Killing time" is one such. Its intended (and innocent) meaning is to engage in some activity to help pass the time while waiting for something else to happen—a plane's departure, a guest's arrival, the bell for class to ring. Yet there is that unnecessarily lethal verb—to kill —which bespeaks far more than an innocent diversion to help time pass; which, in fact, says to deaden time. Which is to say to rob time of *life*. We have far too many ways to do this. Among them is letting the past or the future deaden, kill, the present, to rob the present of the life-giving potency of now. Is it merely whimsy to call this a crime?

In exchange for the gift of life, God asks us to *give life* to the precious time we have, not to kill it. What on earth does this mean? Jesus tried to teach us what it meant. Caring about someone gives life to time. So do compassion and forgiveness, plain human decency, the courage to stand up for what we believe in, the willingness to do our best by today, the openness to recognize all the remarkable ways—remarkable because so confoundedly ordinary—that God is actively present to us and our lives each day. Far more than the sun brings light and warmth to our day and welcomes us into it. We no more bring the sun into our day than we do God into our lives. But we can so pollute our air that the sun's presence is scarcely seen or felt; we can so abuse our inner environment that God's presence is scarcely seen or felt. Nothing more kills time than shutting God out of our lives or, rather, trying to do so. God, like the sun, is just there, whether we choose so or not. Thanks be to God.

Living things grow one day at a time. Never, in the entire recorded history of the human race, is there a single instance of a living thing being given even two days to live at once, let alone more. Like it or not, life is given to us one day at a time (one of which is surely going to be our last). If we speak with faith, we say that God gives us life one day at a time, moment by moment. In the face of our deep-down, impatient desire to want it all now, what an extraordinary grace it is to learn to live life as it is given to us, one day at a time; to learn to ask ourselves, "What does today set before me to be taken care of, to be accomplished, to be loved?" This is not some artificial mind game; it is to be in harmony with the true nature of time and life.

Wasn't this what Jesus was trying to teach us when he gave us this to pray: give us this day our daily bread? Not, as our you've-got-to-look-to-the-future selves would have it, a week's supply, a month's supply, a year's supply. No. Just, "give us enough for this day." And the remarkable truth, hidden by all the ways we squander time, is that we are always given enough for today, if we do not waste our resources uselessly on yesterday or tomorrow.

Is it merely coincidence that one and the same word has these three different meanings? Present has the temporal meaning, now; present also means gift; and being present signifies presence. Whether coincidence or not, surely the present moment is gift. But it is a gift received only to the extent we are present to it, only to the extent we give it our loving attention—our presence.

When everything is said and done, there is one overriding reason why it is imperative for us to learn to live in the present. God, who transcends time and space, is a God of here-and-now. God encounters us only in our present. God is not somewhere down the road, waiting for us to catch up to where we could have been, should have been, by now. God waits on us right here, right now. If we are not present here and now, how will the twain ever meet? God is where life is; and life beckons us, always, in our present moment.

The beautiful, if somewhat dismaying, reading from Ecclesiastes that began this chapter tells us there is a time for everything under the sun. Because this is so, life continually holds this question up before us: What is it time for? This question occurs so routinely on the mundane level of everyday living, we scarcely even notice it. What is it time for? It's time to get up. It's time to leave if we are to get there on time. It's time to take the car in for a tune-up. It's time for dinner. Paying sufficient attention to this question shapes our days, allows them to be reasonably orderly, unharried, manageable.

However, across our days this question can come at us on much deeper levels than the details of our daily routine, in ways we fail to hear, though what is at stake is far more than the orderly management of today. What is it time for? It is time to let go of youth and start acting my age. It's time to stop kidding myself and admit I have a problem and go for help. It's time to take stock of my life and ask myself where I'm going. It's time to let go of this job and move on. It's time to give more attention to my family. It's time to give prayer and faith more place in my life. What is it time for?

And there is this about it, too: the question arises anew out of the changed circumstances of each of the stages of our lives. There is no answering it once and for all. The answer that was adequate and served well when we were beginning our careers, when the children were small, when money was scarce, no longer fits when career is fairly in place, children grown, money not a major problem. The answer that seemed right when we were full of energy is no longer quite so right as our energies wane. The answer that worked marvelously for us when everything was going well no longer works when we are in trouble and things aren't going well. Our circumstances keep changing as time goes by; *we* keep changing as time goes by. If we are not paying sufficient attention, we end up trying to use answers that no longer fit and, therefore, no longer work well for us. What is it time for? Life never has done with asking this question of us.

For most of us there is a discrepancy between the values we *profess* and the values we *live*. The size of the discrepancy is probably as good a measure as any of our sinfulness. With God's grace we work at closing the gap, but the gap is still there. Like St. Paul we aim at the better, yet find ourselves doing the less good. For this reason, our professed values are not the most reliable indicator of the values that efficaciously determine how we live our lives. A much more reliable, if less flattering, indicator is this: what do we spend our time on? This is a concrete and verifiable indicator of what, when the chips are down, we effectively value here and now in our lives, and according to what priorities. How do we spend our time?

How much of our lives do we spend on work? on family and friends? on rest and relaxation? on solitude and prayer, on the things of God? Granted not all of this is simply up to us to determine—for example, the hours of work our job requires of us—but much of it is. What we do with the time that is, in fact, at our disposal reveals our priorities. When the man who has no time for his family piously professes that family comes first for him, somehow his protestations ring false. When one professes, "God comes first in my life," and yet gives no time to God, isn't this simply one more self-deception? What we give our time to is synonymous with what we pay attention to. And the simple fact is that we pay little or no attention to what is of no real concern to us. "But there isn't enough time for everything!" Indeed, how true. And precisely because this is true, what we do give our time to is a dead giveaway as to what we value most, as to what comes first for us.

The ongoing challenge, of course, is *balance*. There are, for most of us, many claims on our time—usually too many. As with our external environment, though, the well-being and preservation of our internal environment, the environment of the spirit, depends on balance. We are learning, all too belatedly, that we interfere with the balances of nature to our own peril: our very survival is at risk. When we allow such values as short-term profit, maximum profit, and narrow self-interest to have precedence over the value of preserving and safeguarding our environment, we suffer the continuing erosion and destruction of the environment which makes life possible. Ignoring and abusing the balances on which our internal environments depend is no less destructive of our inner life, the life of the spirit. If we would know how well or how ill we are preserving a life-engendering balance, we have only to look at how we spend our time.

When we look at time with the eyes of faith, we are compelled, ultimately, to look beyond time, beyond the furthest horizon the mind can see or imagine. Even our words for it sound in the ear as color words must sound to one born blind: eternal, forever, timeless, everlasting, without end. No nook or corner of our human experience, immersed in time as it is, sheds light here. And yet Jesus made the promise: our lives will transcend time and death. Neither of these will have the final say. Here, perhaps, most of all, faith can only say, "I believe," not "I understand." When even time is gone God will still be. And as long as God is, so will we be. This is what Jesus promised us.

In the light of what Jesus taught, no reflection on time can be complete without one further consideration.

In every eucharist we pray the Lord to "protect us from all anxiety as we wait in joyful hope for the coming of our Savior, Jesus Christ." Waiting. For all who believe in Jesus, waiting is an aspect of time we're called to remember and reverence.

Few of us are very good at waiting. We avoid it whenever possible, and when it can't be avoided, we fuss and fume our way through it (traffic jams), we try to distract ourselves with magazines, unneeded snacks, daydreams (the hurry-up-and-wait of airports), we pray to God for mercy and forgiveness (dentists' waiting rooms). Waiting, one is tempted to say, is for the birds. It is also, alas, for us, an inescapable part of life. Like it or not, we have to learn how to wait. Waiting is, even more so, an integral part of faith.

Waiting implies expecting. We can hardly be said to be waiting for the arrival of a guest if we are not expecting one to arrive, awaiting the arrival of a letter unless we have reason to think (or, perhaps, hope) a letter is on the way. Expectations and waiting go hand-in-hand. Some of our expectations are wishful, ill-conceived, unrealistic, and these, of course, lead inevitably to disappointment and frustration. "Expect nothing and you'll never be disappointed" may be a formula for a disappointment-free existence, but it is also a formula for despair. To expect nothing is to live without hope.

Hope is what Christian waiting is all about. Hope in the promises of Jesus Christ, the expectation that the Lord lives up to his word. The Lord who promised that not a sparrow falls unnoticed by the Father. The Lord who promised not to abandon us or to leave us to our own devices. The Lord who promised to send the Holy Spirit to dwell in our hearts and souls. The Lord who promised, incredibly, that even sin and death would not have the final say because he was going on to prepare a home for us and then return to take us there. When we look at all

Jesus promised is it not true that our common failing is not that we expect too much, but that we expect far too little?

Jesus promised forgiveness to the repentant heart, and we, unwilling to let go of our guilt, expect only punishment. Jesus promised a Father's providential care in all our affairs, and we, unwilling to let go of control, expect everything to depend solely on our efforts. Jesus promised we would be given enough for today, and we, unwilling to trust, expect there will not be enough for tomorrow. How often Jesus was moved to cry out: O you of little faith! Was he not trying to tell us we expect far too little, hope for much less than the fullness of what he promised?

There is a paradox in this business of Christian waiting: we already have what we're waiting for, if we would but see it. In faith we know the kingdom of God is here and now. In faith we know that we are temples of the Holy Spirit because God's Spirit dwells in us now. In faith we know we have been redeemed by the death and resurrection of Jesus Christ.

We already have this, but not *all* of it. God's kingdom is here, but not in its fullness. God's Spirit dwells in us, making us temples, but the temples are not completed yet. Yes, we have been redeemed, but we are still living out our salvation. We already have it, but not all of it. For this we have to wait. But, thank God, we don't have to sit around twiddling our thumbs while we wait. There's plenty to do in this joint enterprise we share with God.

There is this, also (though who would have dared believe it unless Jesus had revealed it to us?): while we wait for God, God waits for us. Surely it could not have been mere coincidence that the father of the prodigal just happened to be there "to spot his son a long way off" on that one day his son returned. He was there that day, surely, because he went every day to look for his son's return.

Loving father that he was, he never gave up hoping for his son's return one day. He was expecting it. He was waiting for it.

God never forces us. God is always willing to meet us just where we are. So God waits till we're ready. God waits till we're willing. God waits for us to come to our senses.

Our faith tells us that one day, when God asks us to return the gift of life entrusted to us, God will give us life outside of and beyond time. It is only from this perspective of faith and hope that we can appreciate what time is really for. It is for appreciating life and life's gifts, not least of which is ourselves. It's for caring and taking care of each other. It's for letting God more and more into our lives so that we live in God and God lives in us through Jesus and the Holy Spirit.

This is what it's time for. The rest is really secondary. We have to be patient, though. Some things just take time.

Today

Today came, smiling, toward me
Arms laden with brightly wrapped gifts.
And I said, "I'll be with you in just a minute."
You see, I was in this conversation with Yesterday
—I forget exactly what it was all about—
And it went on and on.
I called out to Today,
"I'll be right with you."
Then, when Yesterday finally finished with me
And before I could get back to Today,
Tomorrow barged right up and began talking.
I called out to Today,
"Just give me a few more minutes."
Well, Tomorrow would be satisfied with nothing less

Than dotting all the i's and crossing all the t's—
I forget what it was all about, really.
(You know how Tomorrow can be.)
So I called out to Today,
"Just hang in there."
Tomorrow, satisfied at last, left me.
And I looked up.
And Today was gone.

4. Making Friends with Meetings

Now on the way to Jerusalem he traveled the border between Samaria and Galilee. As he entered one of the villages, ten lepers came to meet him. They stood some way off and called to him, "Jesus, Master! Take pity on us." When he saw them he said, "Go and show yourselves to the priests." Now as they were going away they were cleansed. Finding himself cured, one of them turned back praising God at the top of his voice and threw himself at the feet of Jesus and thanked him. The man was a Samaritan. This made Jesus say, "Were not all ten made clean? The other nine, where are they? It seems that no one has come back to give praise to God, except this foreigner." And he said to the man, "Stand up and go your way. Your faith has saved you"
(Lk 17:11–19).

The gospel accounts are filled with the encounters that occurred between Jesus and the men and women, even the children, who crossed his path. Encounters with such a different feeling from one to another (in what both Jesus and those he encountered felt), encounters with such varied outcomes. Just like our encounters with those whose paths cross ours. If Jesus was, indeed, as human as we are, his day-by-day interactions with other human beings surely affected how he felt about his day, how he felt about being a human being. Isn't this how it is for us? It is primarily our relationships with one another, not with things, that have the power either to nourish or deplete our spirits. Sunsets and puppy dogs, for all their power to lift our spirits and light our hearts, are not what keep us awake nights with worry or, unless we are born to be hermits, fill our hearts. Only people do that.

Of all the criteria Jesus could have singled out to name the indelible and unmistakable trademark of his disciples, the papers that would verify authentic pedigree, he chose this one: the way we treat one another. John put it harshly: "Anyone who says, 'I love God,' and hates his brother, is a liar, since a man who does not love the brother that he can see, cannot love God whom he cannot see" (1 Jn 4:20–21). Love has everything to do with how we meet people.

How we meet God is of a piece with how we meet others. How we meet others depends on how we meet ourselves. Which brings us to a consideration of meetings, what they are, what they call out of us, what they have to give or take away from us. Meetings are woven into the fabric of our day-to-day lives. Whether we're aware of it or not, meetings weave the tapestry of what is distinctly human in our existence. They merit our thoughtful attention.

There are many words in our language that are over-burdened, made to carry far more than any one word should. "Meetings" is such a word. A whole gamut of human interactions—indifferent, trivial, forgettable; frustrating, disappointing, upsetting, annoying; profound and transforming—we designate "meetings." It might be helpful to look at some of them.

Introductions are one kind of meeting. "Mary, I'd like you to meet John." "How do you do. My name is Terry. Hello, I'm Tom." If Mary is later asked whether or not she has met John, she can say, "Yes, we've been introduced." Introductions, though called meetings, are barely worthy of the name. We learn one another's name, what we look like, maybe a few bits of information about one another. If they go no further, introductions produce acquaintances, not friends. More accurately, they should be called *potential* meetings. They lay the groundwork for meeting, but only if they go beyond the introductions. They may lead to friendship, but only if they are given a great deal more time and attention and care than we give to acquaintances.

Though it may sound strange to put it this way, many individuals' relationship with *themselves* is best described as an acquaintanceship. They have been, equivalently, "introduced" to themselves by parents, teachers, and others. They know their name, what they look like, a considerable amount of information about themselves. But how do they really feel, what do they really think? What is it like to live inside their skin? What are their deepest dreams, their aspirations, their brokenness? They scarcely know. Spending so much time and attention on what is going on outside of themselves, whether to get along, please others, succeed, they have little time or energy left to pay attention to what is going on inside. They feel themselves not worth their serious attention. The solitude, without which there can be no self-reflection, so easily triggers feelings of loneliness that they avoid solitude. If our innermost selves can be likened to a home, they spend as little time as possible at home. What's at home but empty rooms and loneliness? Virtual strangers to themselves, they are incapable of relationships with others that go much beyond acquaintances. Meeting only in public places—whether these be outside or inside us—hardly permits more than surface meetings.

If we are strangers to ourselves, how can we meet God? God can be, at best, an acquaintance. The Holy Spirit, who makes a home within us, waits in vain to meet us there, if we spend as little time as possible at home within ourselves. The introduction, the potential meeting, is not given any chance to grow beyond that into friendship. And so God's love for us remains a one-sided love.

And so we don't even suspect how much God loves us. The earthen vessel contains a treasure, but we don't even know it's there. It takes time and attention and care to come to know it.

Another kind of meeting is the I-have-a-meeting-to-go-to kind. The PTA, the parish council, the board of directors, the neighborhood association. To be a member of any group is to have meetings to go to. In the best of all possible worlds every meeting would have a published agenda. There would be no hidden agenda. The published agenda would actually be followed, would be what the meeting was about. Everyone present could speak and, since all would say what they really meant, they would be listened to with respect and taken seriously. There would be no politicking, no maneuvering for advantage, no manipulation of the participants. The meeting would actually accomplish that which it was called to do, a reasonable disposition of the items on the agenda to the satisfaction of the participants. Meetings would begin and end on time. Even, occasionally, in the course of the meeting the participants would truly encounter one another in mutual trust and respect. This is not the best of all possible worlds.

If we stop to think about it, do we not frequently attend such meetings within ourselves? All those diverse parts of ourselves (none of which, be it pointed out, did we choose for ourselves) convene to claim our attention, seek our vote, win our sympathy. On one side of that inner conference table, duty, responsibility, the right-thing-to-do, sit so sternly, in all their unassailable majesty, even though their credentials do not bear too close inspection. Their arrogance is the tyrant's, their power is the guilt they dispense so freely. On the other side of that table, in places equally privileged, sit the representatives of ego: ambition, accomplishment, success, recognition. Reason is seated at the head of the table, presumably to preside, but so easily overwhelmed by the voices seated immediately right and left. And down toward the other end of the table, far from the ear of reason, those softer voices of self, those truest voices of self: genuine human needs, instinct, intuition, imagination, creativity, to name a few. So often they go unheard, unattended in the clamor around that table. And faith—what voice is given to faith in this inner conference room, the softest voice of all? For among all that is present there, waiting to be asked to speak and be heard, is the Holy Spirit. As we meet ourselves in this inner conference room, are we even aware that God waits to be heard around that table, speaking in a voice not our own?

There are meetings that may be described as the daily, garden variety sort of meetings. The face or faces that look back at ours across the breakfast table, those with whom we work or who work for us, the clerk in the store, a neighbor dropping by, someone who smiles or says hello passing on the street. All those who, in one way or another, encounter the fact of our existence on earth, and we theirs, as we make our way through our day.

These daily sightings of other human beings may barely register on the screen of our awareness, may be no more than fleeting glimpses of one another, scarcely noticed overlappings of our living space with theirs, and theirs with ours, but they can say more about us than we care to think.

How do we treat those whose lives, howsoever briefly, touch ours? With courtesy and respect? Or are these saved selectively for those we consider important? There are people who consider themselves paragons of social grace and who, perhaps, are so charming with those they consider "one of them," but who are blind to the rudeness, not to say contempt, with which they treat others— waiters, clerks, children, employees—whom they consider their inferiors. There are people who manage to make even momentary encounters unpleasant. Just as there are those whose courtesy and kindness, whose smile, whose friendliness somehow renew one's faith in the human race. How we encounter these mostly anonymous others whose paths cross ours each day is our contribution to the quality of human life. Our contribution may seem no more than the widow's mite, hardly worth giving; but we know what Jesus had to say about that.

Then there are mediated meetings. "I'm so glad to meet you. I've heard so much about you!" The meeting is mediated by what one has already heard, positive or negative, about the person one is meeting. When the meeting has been mediated, one inevitably brings to the meeting preconceived ideas, biases, assumptions based on what one has heard. All of which interfere with first meetings. Unless these preconceived ideas are gotten out of the way and the others are allowed to speak for themselves, there is small chance of meeting others as they really are. Self-revelation is a slow and timid process for all of us. We need all the help we can get. Preconceived ideas about us, positive no less than negative, can scare us back into the shells we wear to protect ourselves. Mediated meetings don't help matters any.

And yet, is this not how we first meet ourselves? Long before we have the maturity to think and speak for ourselves, to form our own opinions, we are told all kinds of things about ourselves, from parents and teachers, from the preacher in the pulpit, from society, from peers: you're good/you're bad; you're smart/you're dumb; you're strong/you're weak; you're attractive/you're ugly. All the blanks are filled in for us. As if on tapes stored within us, these voices can play back at us all our lives, preventing us from ever meeting the far from perfect but fairly decent human being we are. Unless we learn how to disconnect the tapes and learn how to allow our inner selves to speak to us, so that we hear *our own* voice, we deal only with others' versions of who we are.

Unfortunately for a life of faith, our initial meeting with God is also a mediated meeting. Before we have learned to recognize the ways God speaks within us, and so before Father, Son, and Holy Spirit are given a chance to reveal themselves to us, we have been told all kinds of things about God. One can choose from any number of versions: God as the infinitely remote and equally uncaring abstraction of some philosophies; God as capricious Santa Claus/magician in the sky; God as stern, punitive, angry judge, to be appeased or else! God as chief executive officer, waiting for you to give your report on your department's productivity, more interested in the profits of the corporation than in your well-being. To name a few. None of these are compatible with the infinitely loving, compassionately involved Father revealed by Jesus but, as with so much else that Jesus taught, we have been infected by the spurious versions. If anyone ever had grounds for libel, surely God does!

When asked by Moses what name he preferred to go by, God said, "I Am who I Am," and then even more simply, "I Am" (Ex 3:13–14). Is it too much to suppose that God had reservations about all those predicate nouns and predicate adjectives we were to attach to that simple I Am? Alongside those internal tapes each of us carries within which tell us who we are, according to others, there is a corresponding set telling us who God is, according to others. Both are the result of mediated meetings. If the tapes are ever to be erased, only direct meeting will do it.

Direct meetings are the only ones that fully deserve to be called meetings. These are the genuine human encounters—immensely joyous, painful, complicated, mysterious, exhilarating, exasperating, tragic, comic—that come from love and lead to love. These are the encounters that beget friends. Somehow these meetings achieve a connection the others fail to do.

In these encounters there is a sense of hearing and being heard, of understanding and being understood. The sense of connection, unlike with acquaintances, goes far beyond the surface and reaches down into much deeper

levels. Friends give each other permission to be themselves and to dispense with the need to impress, convince,
justify. In these encounters, words, when they need to be
used at all, seem able to do what they're supposed to do:
point beyond themselves to the *experience*, for which
there are no words. In contrast to the always painful experience of being put-up-with, tolerated, patronized, in these
encounters one experiences being received and welcomed
with respect and truthfulness. It's a come-as-you-are experience; we are made neither more nor less than we are.

In these encounters feelings of loneliness, separate-
ness, and isolation may not be completely banished, but
they relax their iron grip, and they are shown up for what
they are: only a sometime part of our human experience,
not all of it. We share the very inner experience which,
unshared, isolates us; we share the privacy we otherwise
need to survive in this world but which, unshared, keeps
us separate and alone; we share even the brokenness,
confusion and frailty that are part of each of us and
which, unshared, can never be healed.

This brief and very incomplete description of human
encounters is meant only to suggest why these are the
only meetings fully worthy of the name.

In the gospel accounts Jesus met all kinds of people
in widely different circumstances—one-on-one and in
crowds, friendly and hostile, sophisticated and simple,
those in positions of power and the least important in his
society. These accounts have much to teach us about
meetings. In them we can see that Jesus practiced what
he preached.

There is really no reason, though, to proceed with this
unless we are willing to accept the *whole* truth of Jesus,
including that part of it which has been a stumbling block
from the beginning: Jesus was as fully human as we are,
with the sole exception of sin. The incarnation was not
some sleight-of-hand, some divinely inspired masquerade
that would allow God to slip into our midst incognito. The

words of John's gospel thunder down the ages in their undeniable intent: "The Word was made flesh, he lived among us" (Jn 1:14).

There are some things that are all or nothing. The humanity of Jesus is one of them. Either he was one of us or he wasn't; either we believe it or we don't. There is no room to hedge here. There is no "say when," as we do when someone is pouring coffee into our cup, or putting a portion of food on our plate. "Say when," meaning, "Tell me when you have enough." Jesus either had *all* of our humanity or none of it. Anything else separates us forever from what he had to teach us about being human and makes the incarnation nothing more than a cruel hoax. Anything else makes Jesus an impostor. If our faith does not totally embrace the humanity of Jesus, there is no way it can embrace our own. And, even with faith, it is difficult enough to embrace and come to terms with our own humanity.

Only a Jesus who bore the full burden of humanity that we bear can teach us anything about meeting others in our broken humanity, which is the only way we can. The gospels can and do speak to our human experience because they grew out of the human experience of Jesus and those who witnessed what happened.

With an understandable concern to preserve the teachings of Jesus, the gospel writers generally focus on what he taught, filling in the scene with a few deft lines, the way an artist can depict a face, an expression, with an economy that leaves it to the eye of the beholder to fill in the details to see the whole. So the gospels leave it up to us, looking with the eyes of the heart out of our own human experience, to read what lies between the lines, what is only suggested or implied. For instance, Luke's gospel tells us only, "His mother stored up all these things in her heart" (Lk 2:52). Yet, what mother who has ever watched her child grow, who has known the sheer helplessness of being unable to shield and protect her child from hurt, who hopes the world for her child, does not know what Mary held in her heart? Their own hearts tell them.

We owe to John's gospel the meeting between Jesus and a Samaritan woman by a well one hot and dusty noontime. John notes that Jesus was tired; he had been journeying and he was tired. If ever anyone encountering Jesus had three strikes against her, here was one! She was a Samaritan: Jews were not supposed to be on speaking terms with Samaritans. She was a woman: in the society of Jesus' day women were considered one of the household possessions. And, like those batters who cannot resist swinging at whatever comes over the plate, she had been married a grand total of five times. And yet, as he always did, Jesus brushed stereotypes aside; he let her speak for herself. He initiated the conversation; there could have been none if he had not taken the initiative. A simple request—he asked her for what she had to give: a drink of water to a thirsty man. She was understandably confused and flustered. Yet, step by step, Jesus gently led her to recognize her own thirsty heart, and what he had to give to her. With compassion and understanding, without a hint of condescension or condemnation, Jesus met her just as she was. Because she was open to it, he shared with her the truth of who he was. The meeting transformed her heart. Like a couple of Marys and an unnamed adulteress, she was to know how quickly the barriers of a bruised and battered heart fell before simple kindness, how another's respect could give back self-respect, how another's willingness honestly to share his truth opened her to her own. She became an apostle to the Samaritans, this unnamed woman who will forever be known as the woman at the well.

This encounter, with its happy outcome, was typical of how Jesus met others, even when the outcome was not so happy. Jesus knew the outcome was not his sole responsibility, that it was equally up to those he met, depending on their response. So the outcomes of his meetings ran the full range from out-and-out rejection to wholehearted acceptance. Fairly like ours.

The time was not high noon but evening. The place was not outdoors but an upper chamber in a house in Jerusalem. The twelve principal participants thought they were meeting Jesus to celebrate the seder meal of the Passover, as indeed they were. But for how very much more than this, they did not realize until much later. This had to be one of the strangest farewell banquets ever. Jesus had tried to warn them, to prepare them for it, but as it turned out, he was the only one aware that this was farewell. Moreover, instead of the departing guest of honor receiving gifts, it was he who gave the farewell gift in the breaking of the bread and the passing of the cup.

He was their leader. For three years they had heard him preach, witnessed the awesome power of this man, the authority that moved hearts and wrought other miracles. If any man had a claim to the leader's prerogatives, surely he did; and they were more than ready to accord them. Yet, while they were at table, this man, their acknowledged leader, went among them washing and drying their feet, a task assigned to servants. Peter, who knew something of the gruff and tumble ways of leading men, was horrified at this lapse of dignity. Leaders don't do this! Leaders were to be served, not serve. How else could one hold respect and maintain authority, unless by lording it over those who are led? This was the fixed way of authority, a wisdom followed from time immemorial. Peter objected strenuously. Jesus would not be deterred; he was adamant. And so he left one more farewell gift for his followers: service, not power, is the coin of that realm which was God's on earth. The greater were to serve the lesser, the strong serve the weak. A new wisdom he left them. They learned, and lived it. And handed it down to us. Have we learned? Do we live it?

Always he met others in the circumstances in which

they found themselves. Publicans and sinners in their haunts (thus acquiring a reputation for carousing with low-life types). Simon and Peter, James and John, fishermen, among their nets, boats, their lakeside. Matthew, tax collector, by the custom house. Nicodemus, at night and unobserved, because Nicodemus feared what his peers would say if they saw him talking with Jesus. Meeting them on their own ground, he beckoned them beyond their own ground to a world of possibilities they'd scarcely dared dream. In each case it was he who believed in them long before they came to believe in him. He was willing to trust them, to accept them, to respect them before they had these to give in return. Seeing more in them than they could see in themselves, he freed them to be more than they thought they were. He wasn't merely showing them who he was, he was showing them who *they* were.

This is the Jesus who meets *us* each day. There is a difference, though. The deal may not be fair, by our standards, but it's the only deal he made with us. He meets us wearing faces not his own and speaking in voices not his own. He meets us in the guise of everyone who crosses our path each day. Lest we harbor any doubts as to how terribly true this is, Jesus wrapped God's final judgment of us around this. "Lord, when did we see you hungry and give you to eat? . . . I tell you solemnly, insofar as you did this to one of the least of these brothers or sisters of mine, you did it to me" (Mt 25:35–40).

We are to give an account of our stewardship over the gift of our life when our sojourn here on earth is done. We have not been left in the dark to guess what we will be asked. In fact, it will not be any of the things we would guess, left to figure it out on our own, not any of the things we consider so important in our judgments of ourselves. Were you successful? Did you accomplish great things? Were you filled with every virtue, did you overcome every shortcoming? No, none of these. Only this:

was there more love or less on earth because you were there? more faith or less? more hope or less? Only this.

The only true wisdom is to see as God sees. We needn't wait until our life is done for this. We don't even have to go out searching for God so we can see. God comes to us. Every day. Both to give and receive. In our every meeting.

Like Some Conversations

Blah blah glah-de-blah.
I don't think so, nah.

Zip zip zippety-doo.
That's an interesting point of view.

Gobbledy bobbley gobbledy crunch.
Don't you think it's time for lunch?

Blather blather blather splat.
Yes, I've always thought that.

Grumble, rumble, bumble pow.
Well, not just right now.

Clankety clankety clankety ka-bang.
It's great being part of this gang.

Blimpety blimpety blimpety-poo.
Yes, well nice talking to you . . .

5. Making Friends with "I Want"

". . . and the truth will set you free" (Jn 8:32).

It may sound strange, even offensive, when put this way, but the best evidence surely suggests that truth and freedom are acquired tastes, perhaps not so esoteric as caviar or pickled eels, but nonetheless requiring careful cultivation. Rhetoric and flag-waving and other touched-up self-portraits would have every human breast aflame with the desire to be free, every mind hungering for the truth. The evidence, as was said, just doesn't support this flattering version of ourselves. What the evidence does support is the sheer ingenuity we can bring to bear to evade entirely or at least doctor the truth, trimming it down to manageable size. And the same with freedom: a little bit goes a long way. Hardly flattering, but there it is: truth and freedom are laboriously acquired tastes.

How often we hear someone say, "I can't just tell him the *truth!*" The reservations are not groundless. Simply telling the truth as one sees it is not one of the prescribed ways to win friends and influence people. All too often we don't want to hear the truth. "How are you?" is a conventional form of greeting, seldom if ever a seriously intended inquiry as to another's health or well-being. Diplomacy, tact, prudence, consideration—do these not also serve as cover for double-talk, evasion, whitewashing, sheer gobbledygook? Without giving it a second thought we learn to tiptoe around unpleasant truths, inconvenient truths, troublesome truths. Equally without much thought we learn to say the things that others want to hear, the *lingua franca* of polite conversation, of civilized manners. Children, who haven't yet learned any better, can bring adult company to an embarrassed silence by blurting out the truth. "She's fat!" "He smells funny!" The silence is usually broken by something like "Children have no manners these days!" or a parental "Don't be rude!" So we learn that it is not polite to tell the truth. The closer to home the truth comes, the less ardently we burn to know it. We may be consumed with curiosity about what, exactly, is going on in the house next door, but our curiosity about what, exactly, is going on in our own hearth and home is strangely, sometimes disastrously, muted. The more our favorite convictions, our cherished opinions, our rational scheme of things are threatened by the truth, the less irresistibly compelling truth becomes. For all our professed readiness to have a spade called by its given name, to do so indiscriminately more often than not catapults us into more than we bargained for. No, the evidence hardly supports the thesis that every mind hungers to know the truth, whatever it may be. The mind's digestive system has to be carefully nurtured and developed if raw truth is to be palatable. No less carefully, honesty and humility need nurturing for the same reason. These, too, are acquired tastes, hardly as common as we like to think.

While we may reluctantly admit, when sufficiently nudged, that, yes, we do tend to play fast and loose with the truth (after all, we have to get along, don't we?), when it comes to freedom, that's a different matter entirely. To suggest that anyone of sound mind does not want freedom is, on the face of it, absurd, perhaps slightly treasonous. The very democracy in which we are blessed to live, with its cherished and hard won freedoms, freedoms we have fought to preserve, gives the lie to any such suggestion. Every red-blooded American is proof to the contrary. But *are* we? If we look beyond the myths and the Fourth of July rhetoric of politicians, what do we really see? When we look inside ourselves, what do we really see?

Yes, if human freedom involved no more than being without external constraints, we all readily fall in line for our share. We chafe at external constraints. We don't like someone else telling us what we may and may not do, where we may and may not go. We don't want someone else running our lives for us. Or so we say. Is not the dream of every adolescent adulthood, which, by definition, is the time when *they* won't be around anymore with all their restrictions, telling us what to do? We may, for the common good (which includes our own), tolerate certain constraints on our freedom, for instance, the freedom to drive on whichever side of the road takes our fancy, at whatever speed we like; but these constraints are seen as necessary evils. Give a little to get a little. Any reprise of Eden in which we have any say would certainly include absence from *all* external constraints. Of course we all want to be free! Any suggestion to the contrary is plainly sinister.

If freedom from external constraints were all there were to it, if this were the essence of human freedom, we could rest our case here. Yes, indeed, we all hunger to be free human beings. But human freedom involves far more than the absence of external constraint. We pay so much attention to the constraints that come from outside us, we scarcely even notice that the real limitations of our freedom come from within and are mostly of our own making. We pound on the doors of our cells and rattle the bars, making a righteous show of outrage at our imprisonment, and all the while the key to the cell rests snugly in our pocket, whether our cell be loneliness and isolation; a life without meaning or purpose; rage that obliterates every other emotion; a lifetime sentence to success, amassing money, being owned by our possessions; a victimhood whose chief perpetrator is *us*. The ages-old tactic still works: concentrate on the enemy without, and you don't have to come to grips with the enemy within. *We* are the chief saboteurs of our freedom. How could we be so lethally effective at it, if we really wanted to be free? And so the case does not rest here.

Thieves break into a home, tie the owner to a chair, rob the house and flee. A neighbor comes by and unties the owner, removes the ropes that constrain his freedom of movement. But what if the man has nowhere he wants to go, nothing he wants to do? It's clear enough what he's been freed *from*—those ropes tying him to the chair. But what has he been freed *for?* Untying the ropes doesn't give him anywhere to go, anything to do. Wanting nothing, he may as well have stayed tied to the chair. What are we free *for?* Here is the crux of human freedom.

Removing external constraints does not settle the problem of human freedom, it merely focuses it, uncovers the real problem and shows it for what it is. The real problem of human freedom is knowing what we really want (truth) and authentically wanting what we want, which is to say, wanting it wholeheartedly, singlemindedly, and without reservation (freedom). Knowing what we really want *is* the truth that will set us free. But, if there's nothing we really want all that much, there's nothing to know.

When we look only to the surface, we say: but everyone wants *something*. We need to look below the surface. We also need to adjust the focus dial so that what we're looking at isn't blurred and fuzzy. We need to separate "I wish," "I feel like," "I would like," from "I want."

"I wish" ushers us into the realm of fairy tales and magic. "I wish life weren't so difficult." "I wish I were more consistent." "I wish I could have it all now and be done with it." "I wish I had a Ph.D." I wish . . . Wishes are the stuff of dreams, wish-fulfillment, the stuff of magic. As long as wishes remain only wishes, there is no bridge between them and reality. The wonderful thing about daydreams as needed respites from the sometimes too-muchness of reality is that daydreams make our every wish come true: everyone is Superman/Superwoman in daydreams. The pathological potential of daydreams is that they become substitutes for reality. The essence of all magic is illusion: magic entices us to misperceive what is in front of our eyes. Romantic ballads notwithstanding, wishing definitely does *not* make it so. The difference between "I wish" and "I want" is the difference be-tween dreams and illusions on the one hand, and reality on the other.

"I feel like" ushers us into those parts of ourselves where impulse, emotion, appetite hold sway. "I feel like taking the day off." "I feel like getting drunk." "I feel like telling him off." "I feel like going out for pizza." These are valuable parts of ourselves and well worth making friends with. They have much to tell us about ourselves, they are the wellsprings of spontaneity and play, and they have much to do with laughter and fun. They are wonderful servants, but they are tyrannical, mindless masters. There is a world of difference between spontaneity and blind, unbridled impulse, between what we may feel like doing and the appropriateness, not to say legality, of doing it, between feelings of the moment and enduring emotional commitments. There is a world of dif-ference between what we may feel like doing and what we want to do.

The mother, sitting by the bed of her sick child at night, dead tired after a full day's work, certainly *feels like* going to bed and getting a good night's sleep. What she *wants*, though, is to be with her sick child in case she is needed. "I feel like" shares much more in common with "I wish" than it does with "I want." "I want" bespeaks a commitment that is lacking in "I feel like."

"I would like" ushers us to the waiting room outside of "I want," but doesn't quite get us in the door. The very language we use betrays the difference. "I would like to lose weight." "I would like to be more kind." "I would like to be a doctor." The subjunctive expresses the reservation, because in all of these there is an *if*: if it doesn't cost too much. "I would like" is still considering the cost before closing the deal. "I would like" is still tentative. It is good and prudent to weigh the cost carefully, to determine first whether one can afford it and, even if one can, whether the price is worth it. "I would like" indicates the matter is under consideration, but still hasn't been decided yet: it can go either way.

"I want" closes the deal, plunks down, if not the full price, the first down-payment. (And are not all life-choices paid for in installments?) And as long as "I want" endures, the payments are made on time. There is a concrete and easily verifiable way to discover for ourselves what it is we really want, as opposed to wishes, what we feel like, or what we would like, if. Embedded in what we do and what we don't do is what we really want. The pre-med major who is taking the required courses and doing the required work can be fairly sure she *wants*, at least as of now, to be a doctor. The man who is following his diet and seeing to it that he does the recommended exercise can truthfully say he *wants* to lose weight. The businessman who does not lie, who does not cheat, has earned the right to say he *wants* to be honest. We can find out rather readily what we want and what we don't by looking at what we do and what we don't do. The method is, while not very flattering to some ideas about ourselves that we cherish, fairly foolproof.

We can deceive ourselves into thinking we want all kinds of things we really don't want. We can mistake what we *should* want for what we really want. We can confuse what others want (or we think they want) for us with what we want for ourselves. We can try to let slip by us all the things we only halfway want and claim them as what we want. Thinking we want them, and frustrated at not getting them, we focus on everything that is getting in the way, blaming circumstances, the placement of the stars, bad luck, and others for our frustration, never suspecting that the real problem is that we really don't want what we think we want.

A freshman presented himself in desperation at the college counseling center one day. He had contracted a strange malady and he had come seeking its cure. His malady was this: he could not study. A good student (an honor student in high school), he'd never had this problem before. He was a pre-med major and knew that he *had* to study for the top grades he would need to get into medical school. He *wanted* to study, but just couldn't make himself study. He was seeking psychological help to find the cure for this affliction that had paralyzed his will. As long as the problem was structured this way, of course, there was no "cure." Instead, the counselor took as his working hypothesis that, in spite of the student's protestations that he wanted to study, he really didn't want to, whatever the reasons. The counselor set out to explore some of the inner world of the student. What emerged in the student's self-revelation, in only a few sessions, was his strong need to try to live up to his father's expectations (as he conceived these), to win his father's praise, to make his father proud of him. His father was, of course, a physician. As he continued to explore he discovered that his own interests and talents did not lie in the field of medicine. A few short steps brought him to see he really didn't want to be a doctor, he really didn't want to study medicine. With no small courage he talked with his father, who proved far more accepting of his son than his son had given him credit for. The student changed his major to one which corresponded with his own interests and talents. His malady disappeared; he was cured! No. There was no malady in the first place. He just thought he wanted something he really didn't want. Once he recognized this, he was back in working order.

Genuine wanting, unlike its spurious look-alikes,

always embraces the means as well as the end. If we really want to get to San Francisco, we take the means to get there. If we really want to do a good job, we give it our best shot. If we really want to be a loving person, we do loving things and we refrain from hateful things. Genuine wanting assesses the price and is willing to pay it. "I really wanted to but . . ." may serve as a more or less convincing alibi, may give aid and comfort to our reluctance to take responsibility, but it doesn't bear too close inspection.

This whole line of thinking about "I want" runs the risk of eliciting such reactions as, "But everyone just can't go around doing what he *wants*," and "If everyone just did his own thing, where would we all be?" Et cetera. In more ways than one we trivialize our wants. As we've seen, we confuse them with "I wish," "I feel like," "I would like to." There is another way we trivialize our wants. Listen to these statements:

> *I want onions on my hamburger.*
> *I want that sweater in yellow.*
> *I want to do well in my studies.*
> *I want to be a good mother.*
> *I want to be a lawyer.*
> *I want to help make this world a better place.*
> *I want to love and serve God in my life.*
> *I want . . . I want . . . I want . . .*

When we reach deeply enough within ourselves, there aren't even words to express all we want, to say the longings and the aspirations of our hearts. By what right does anyone limit the use of the word to the onions-on-hamburger statement, trivializing it? Each statement legitimately expresses some of what we want. Our problem is not that we take our wants too seriously, but that we do not take them nearly seriously enough. We are not willing to pay the full cost. We want somewhat less than wholeheartedly. Our wanting, to say the least, is not all-of-a-piece.

One way to understand why our "I want" is so often less than unequivocal is to return to that inner conference room alluded to in Chapter 4. The amount of wrangling that goes on around that table has much to do with the quality of "I want." After all, it is around that inner table that "I want" is determined. Are *all* the legitimate representatives of self given a fair say in the deliberations?

Are our feelings taken into account? Or do we take the ridiculous position, "Let's be objective; let's keep feelings out of this." Ridiculous because it is no more possible to keep our feelings out than it is to pretend that we are not flesh-and-blood human beings. We may ignore our feelings but, when we do, they simply go underground and operate outside of reasonable control, undermining the decisions in which they were given no say. Or, at the opposite extreme, do we allow our feelings to shout down the other voices in that inner room? In either case, "I want" emerges badly compromised from the start.

Are our authentic human needs taken into account in our decisions? It would be truly wonderful to be without any needs, but that's not how God happened to fashion us. Like it or not, we have needs we ignore to our own peril. We *need* sufficient nourishment and rest—for the spirit as well as the body. We *need* to make some sense of our lives, find some purpose and meaning in it. We *need* a certain measure of gratification in our work, our relationships, our selves—to name just a few needs. Needs do not come under the heading of "optional equipment," nor are they luxury items, to be dispensed with when the crunch is on. We can suffer the deprivation of one or another of our needs for a time without undue damage, true, but prolonged, excessive deprivation wreaks havoc that prevents anything in us from working right. Unless we give our needs their rightful voice in our inner conference room, we are asking for trouble. We may desire to pay the price for what we want, but we'll run out of money to pay it. If, at the opposite extreme, "I want" takes into account no one else's needs but our own, "I want" becomes synonymous with a selfish, me-first (and therefore ultimately self-defeating) enterprise.

Perhaps the two most powerful inner voices around that table (these, after all, are the majority shareholders) are mind and heart. When these two vote as a bloc, they'll win hands down every time. The problem is, they tend to take adversary positions, each envious of the other's prerogatives. Like two people who need each other to stay honest, these two dimensions of ourselves tend to resent each other.

Our minds are truly wonderful, powerful instruments, that which distinguishes us from other two-legged animals. There is still simply no substitute for intelligence. Yet, the utter foolishness and stupidity otherwise intelligent people are capable of is sometimes scarcely to be believed. The games our minds, left to their own devices, can play still put computer games to shame. An "I want" that rests on nothing more than the conclusion of a syllogism, on sheer logic, has scant chance of making it in the real world.

Our hearts are no less wonderful, powerful instruments. The heart knows things the mind alone can never know. The heart sees color where the mind sees only black and white. On its own, the mind can say (sometimes), "I understand," but it can never say, "I love"—it takes the collaboration of the heart to say that. Left to itself, though, the heart is even more adept at foolishness than the mind is. The heart isn't very good at assessing consequences. Even the most heartfelt "I want" that does not have the mind's imput and cooperation proceeds on very shaky legs.

Working in concert, mind and heart can rightly claim credit for the poetry and art we know, for whatever loves enrich our lives. An "I want" jointly sponsored by both mind and heart is the one that stands the best chance of enduring.

Faith tells us there is another voice waiting to be heard from in that inner conference room. We are temples of the Holy Spirit. God's own Spirit speaks within us, enlightening and guiding, inspiring, comforting, and encouraging us. It is, though, a voice that rarely speaks above a whisper. We have to still the other voices and to listen carefully in the stillness to hear this voice. It is not a voice of imperious demand but of gentle invitation. We have to be open and willing if we are to heed it. It is, more than all of the other voices put together, the voice of truth and goodness speaking within us. For it is God speaking within us. To hear and recognize that voice, to give it our wholehearted yes, is to follow where God wants to lead us. Here, finally, is where "I want" and "God wants" can become one.

Even granting that our "I want" is all-of-a-piece, that we are willing, with God's grace, to pay all the costs, there is no money-back guarantee that we will achieve everything we want. That's the risk. Our best efforts sometimes are just not enough. There is much that is simply beyond our power to control, including the response of others. Much more than our own efforts, our own good will, even our own dedication, is involved in the process that leads to any goal we set ourselves. The risk is disappointment, pain, sometimes even a broken heart. Facilely to trot out at this point, "Better to have tried in vain than not to have tried at all," is downright fatuous. For whatever truth it might contain, it in no way lessens the very real and potentially devastating risk of things not working out. All of us have to make the choice for ourselves; no one else can do it for us. Each of us has to face that terrifying prospect: what if, after giving it our all, it just doesn't work out? To leave the element of risk out of the equation whose central value is "I want" is to do violence to the truth. This risk, after all, *is* part of the price. We do ourselves no favor in minimizing the risk.

But isn't this whole business of "I want" open to abuse? Psychopaths *want* to rape and kill, and they do. All of us, sinners, can want what is wrong, do what is wrong —destructive, unloving, greedy, hateful, cruel. Our corporate history reads like a horror story. Doesn't all of this come from people just doing what they want to do? What can one say to this objection? Only this: *life* is open to abuse but that is hardly a reason for denying life. And this, too: ultimately, we have to take the objection up with God. God, of all people, had to know our capacity to abuse the gift of freedom, and yet God offered the gift anyway. Perhaps this has something to do with it: love is either freely given or it is not love. Maybe that's why God is willing to risk all the abuses: to give us a chance at love. If this is so, apparently God thinks the risks are worth it. Do we?

Knowing what we really want and going for it is what freedom is *for*—is, in fact, the heart and soul of human freedom. The more tentative and confused we are about what we really want, the less freedom we enjoy. The more wholeheartedly we want what we want, the more committed to it we are, the more freedom we enjoy. Contrary to popular opinion (where freedom is confused with license, where an uncritical "go with the flow" epitomizes the free spirit, and commitment is equated with tying oneself down), dedication—which is to say, giving oneself entirely—is what human freedom is *for*.

Jesus gave his life to free us from bondage. No one gave more to win our freedom than he did. No one knew more about freedom of spirit than he did. And how did he sum up all of the law and commandments? How did he define and live the way, the truth, and the life? Just this: Love your God with your whole mind and heart and love one another as God loves you. Love is the key to the door of the cell, whatever it may be, that keeps us unfree.

Fearing its responsibilities, we hedge the awesome possibilities of loving wholeheartedly. And yet it remains true: only the heart that has given all that it has to give knows the fullness of human freedom. The way Jesus did.

Create in Me a New Heart

Create in me a new heart, Lord
Where there is pride and anger,
Petty selfishness and stinginess,
Fear and frenzied clutching,
A strident voice clamoring
Me, me, and me,
Let there be your humble gentleness,
Your generous spirit,
Your calm and trusting faith.
Let my inner voice cry out
For You, and only You.

Gather the scattered pieces
Of my heart, Lord,
Broken up by too much hungering,
Too much hankering after
Substitutes for You, for me;
Too much cosmetic,
Counterfeit—and costly—
Dallying with tinsel, froth,
Bargain-basement loves,
And economy-size contentment
With mediocrity.

Clear out the clutter
Of my heart, Lord,
The years' accumulation
Of worn-out desires,
And used-up hopes,

No-longer-working wishes,
Faded memories and
Mismatched pairs of dreams.
A garage sale?
Dear Lord, no! It's junk—
Worthless, wasted wanting.

Oh, Lord, how hard to pray so!
You see, the coward in me
Prays otherwise;
Prays that pain be gone,
And disappointments,
And all those bruisings of the heart
That follow love,
That measure love.
So hear the coward, too,
But, hearing, heed Your heart's
Own answer to me.

6. Making Friends with Holiness

"You must therefore be perfect as your heavenly Father is perfect" (Mt 5:48).

Idealism is a tricky business. On the one hand, ideals are like the North Star; they give us a sense of direction relative to true north in our lives. Ideals are a constant reminder to us that more is possible if we would but reach out for it, that we are, with God's grace, capable of being better than we are, that there is always room for improvement. Our ideals energize our efforts to look for better ways to do what we do; they are our hedge against complacency and an easy partnership with mediocrity. Ideals prompt us to go the extra mile, to set aside the nay-saying voices, to reach within and find the resources we otherwise would never know are there. Ideals are the foundation upon which believing in ourselves and our possibilities rests, keeping faith with ourselves and not settling for expediency, the coward's compromise, the cynic's pragmatism. Ideals represent what the best and the brightest in each of us long for, hope for, dare to try for. Fated for this because, as Augustine put it: "Our hearts, O Lord, are made for you and they will not rest till they rest in you." Without ideals we are like a ship without a rudder in an exceedingly storm-tossed sea.

On the other hand (*why* does there always have to be that other hand?), ideals are, by definition, unobtainable, never to be fully realized. Ideals hold before us possibilities, none of which can ever be achieved to perfection this side of the grave. The North Star is there to show travelers true north, not to serve as their *destination* (at least not this far into the space age). By their very nature ideals always lie beyond, ahead of what is here and now in ourselves and our lives, just around that corner we never reach; they always point to *more* than actually is. Ideals represent what, with the grace of God, can be for us, not what is.

All this being so, the possibilities for mischief are many, most of which we have duly discovered and exploited in one way or another, causing ourselves and others much needless anxiety, pain, and frustration. How do we do this? Let us count the ways.

When we choose to forget that genuine ideals can never be fully realized, our idealism is transmogrified into perfectionism. For the perfectionist, obviously, nothing less than perfection is ever good enough, in oneself, in others. For the matriculating perfectionist, in spite of deplorable (i.e. imperfect) teachers, a GPA of less than 4.0 is totally unacceptable. For the salesman perfectionist, anything less than the Top Salesman of the Year Award is dismal failure. For the religious perfectionist, anything less than the fullness of grace is moral disaster and spiritual bankruptcy. Quite simply, the perfectionist has impossible expectations along with their concomitantly impossible demands. Impossible because ideals can never be fully realized. The perfectionist, to put it kindly, is a great pain to self and to others.

The surface manifestations of and the basic formula for perfectionism are fairly straightforward: perfection or nothing. Not nearly so straightforward are the below-the-surface inner workings of perfectionism, the conceit and deceit going on in the murky depths of it. On the surface perfectionism appears to be a too lusty appetite for the perfect, an over-dosing on the ideal, a too zealous dedication to improvement, to goodness, to holiness. And for these reasons we tend to think of perfectionism as something *more* than "ordinary" idealism, a kind of severe case of idealism, a kind of nine-foot-two genetic aberration of idealism. The real truth of it can be seen only when we look below the surface.

Perfectionists, in reality, fear failure so much they dare not risk it. What better way to avoid the risk than a built-in alibi, a made-to-order-and-guaranteed *explanation* for failing? If failure is inevitable and unavoidable, one can hardly be held to blame for it. If success is precluded in advance, there *is* no risk; the outcome is a foregone conclusion. And, again, hardly the fault of the innocent aspirant. And how to do this? Simple: pick goals that are, by any sane reckoning, impossible for *anyone* to attain. Then we need not look to ourselves for the inevitable failure, the *guaranteed* failure; we can look to the goals: we didn't fail them, they failed us—by being impossible to achieve. After all, impossibility lets anyone off the hook. All this perfectionists gain by, ostensibly, "forgetting" that ideals are, by their very nature, unobtainable. Contrary to all appearances, the perfectionist is not willing to take the risk of failing. Perfectionism is not something more than idealism; it is something far, far less. For it is precisely our ideals that empower us to risk what we otherwise would not dare.

In addition to sparing us the risk of failure, perfectionism has other fringe benefits. Perfectionism offers us license to be dissatisfied with everyone and everything (since, obviously, there is nothing perfect in this life). The perfectionist is forever asking, "Is that *all*?"

There are degrees of dissatisfaction, of course. Idealism carries as an item on its price-tag a certain dissatisfaction. For instance, the restless heart to which Augustine alludes. A restless heart, yes, a heart wanting more than all this world has to give, wanting, in fact, nothing less than God—and so of course dissatisfied. But nonetheless a *loving* heart. Wanting more does not prevent us from loving what we already have, imperfect as it is; does not prevent us from giving all of ourselves to the present reality of our lives. In fact, wanting more not only does not prevent us from loving what we already have, but there can't be the one without the other: we can truly want more of what we have only to the extent that we love what we have. If we find a half-cup of fermented mango juice thoroughly distasteful, by what insane logic do we convince ourselves we're going to find the full cup ambrosial?

Consider a man who holds his newborn son in his arms and says to him: "Come back to me when you are a full-grown man and then I shall love you, then I will be father to you, and you son to me." He would thereby destroy both fatherhood and sonship, killing the seed that makes growth of the plant possible. If he cannot love the infant, the toddler, the child, the adolescent, what magic will bestow on him the ability to love the man?

In a somewhat earlier time, here is how John said it less cautiously in one of his letters: "Anyone who says, 'I love God,' and hates his brother, is a liar, since a man who does not love the brother that he can see cannot love God, whom he has never seen" (1 Jn 4:20–21). If we find ourselves simply incapable of cherishing the less than complete manifestations of God's presence in our midst, the less than full measures of caring, fumbling good will, stumbling generosity, tentative and shy moves toward reconciliation, frightened willingness to give it another try, honest failure—all of the fragile stirrings of life and spirit in ourselves and others, in this real world we inhabit—by what insane logic do we convince ourselves that we truly want the full measure? No. Loving what might be or can be begins with the admittedly daunting struggle to love what *is*. Surely, God's example should have taught us that much after all this time!

Not so for full-fledged perfectionists. Their license exempts them from all this. Their dissatisfaction with anything exempts them from all this. Their dissatisfaction with anything less than perfect makes it impossible for them to love *anything* they find. Their hearts are not restless, they are dead. Their dissatisfaction has nothing to do with wanting more or loving, it is their exit visa from the human race. Having tested the human race and found it wanting, they have decided not to renew their membership therein. Their over-riding dissatisfaction can shrivel anyone it touches: a spouse, an offspring, a would-be friend, a co-worker, an employee, just about anyone. Because a far more accurate name for their dissatisfaction is contempt. Love, howsoever imperfect, is life-giving; contempt and its effects are love's polar opposite. Contempt is an acid which destroys human flesh and spirit unless it is washed off as quickly and thoroughly as possible. The ultimate tragedy of perfectionists is this: there is no one with whom they are more dissatisfied than themselves, no one for whom they have more contempt than themselves. Others catch only the overflow.

Perhaps it's an offshoot of perfectionism (it certainly shares much in common with it), perhaps it's another mischief deserving of its own name. Whichever, it is another way we are capable of changing the ideals which free us to be more into shackles that bind and diminish us. We do this when we substitute *our* definition of perfection for God's, our concept of holiness for the holiness God calls each of us to put on.

The concept of holiness we concoct for ourselves is largely ego-inspired. (Ego is that facet of our psyche which, not content with imaging God, is forever trying to *play* God.) To be holy is to be successful, spiritually successful, of course. To be holy is to achieve, spiritual achievement, of course. To be holy involves acquisition, the acquisition of virtues, of course. To be holy involves competition, spiritual competition, of course. To be holy is to be in control and on top of things, so it means we must eliminate every weakness and vulnerability, or anything else that stands in the way of our succeeding, spiritually, of course. In a word, to be holy is simply to take that true-grit, right-stuff, let's-get-the-job-done approach that works so well in the marketplace and related enterprises, baptize and confirm it, and set it loose in the realm of the spirit. The bottom line of ego-inspired holiness is this: my holiness is something *I* both define and accomplish.

Is this God's idea of holiness as revealed to us by Jesus Christ? Long before Jesus, Isaiah foresaw the answer: ". . . for my thoughts are not your thoughts, my ways are not your ways—it is Yahweh who speaks. Yes, the heavens are as high above the earth as my ways are above your ways, my thoughts above your thoughts" (Is 55:8-9). God, for all our anthropocentric ways of bracketing God, never has gone about things the way we would have, if the written record and our experience are any indication. Not only is God not contained in any of our human categories, the best evidence seems to bear out Isaiah: our thoughts are somewhat at variance with God's. (For which we should be eternally grateful.) God writes straight with crooked lines, the old proverb puts it. The crooked is ours, the straight is God's.

When Jesus enjoined us to be perfect as our heavenly Father is perfect, he made it painfully clear he was talking about love. His life, his whole message was about love and the healing, redeeming power of love. First of all, God's incredible love for us, and only consequently our love for God, which is inseparable from our love for one another. Jesus gives us only one criterion by which we have any right to be called his followers, only one criterion by which we will be judged by God in the final accounting of our lives: the love we showed one another and how we took care of one another's needs. Paul got the message: "God chose us in [Jesus] before the world began, to be holy and blameless in his sight, to be full of love" (Eph 1:4). In *his* sight, not ours. John got the message also: "Anyone who fails to love can never have known God, because God is love . . . as long as we love one another God will live in us and his love will be complete in us" (1 Jn 4:8,12).

Genuine holiness is God's Holy Spirit living within us. This is the only holiness that is of God. It wears faces as varied as ours from one another, as many as the faces of love. They are scattered across the pages of the gospels: the no-nonsense directness of the good Samaritan, the unobtrusive, shy mite of the widow, Peter's gruff and headstrong dedication, the tears of Magdalene. They are scattered, too, across the pages of our lives, if we have but eyes to see. We do well not to tamper with what Jesus told us of holiness, what he showed us of holiness.

And, finally, our holiness is the work of the Holy Spirit within us—God's accomplishment, not ours. Holiness is a gift to be received, not a task to be achieved. True, it is up to us to open our hearts to receive the gift. We can say yes or no to it, as we can always say yes or no to love. We can take care of the gift or abuse it. That's our part in the enterprise. The gift and its giving is God's. Thanks to the gift of God, we are called to image the heart of God. This is the only true holiness.

Given our incorrigible ingenuity, there is yet another way we can do mischief in the name of idealism and holiness, another way we can evade responsibility. This brings us once again to the difference between the ideals we *profess* and the ideals we *live*. With God's grace we struggle painfully to reduce the difference, little by little. If the struggle proves too much, though, there is another way out for us. We can insulate our ideals so they don't interfere with and complicate our lives, we can relegate them to the realm of the "ideal"—to wit, that utopian realm which has little or nothing to do with the "real," i.e. the realities of life. Idealism *versus* realism. In this reconstruction, ideals are confined largely to saying the right things and professing the right faith, never mind what one *does*. Idealism as rhetoric. Politicians are the easiest to single out because they are the most public, but they are, after all, only our surrogates. We're the ones who keep electing them. They represent *us*. Idealism as rhetoric, slogans. No one, after all, is expected to take all of this *seriously*. The *real* world, where things get done, is a different matter entirely. The one who confuses the two, who insists that ideals be given a place in the real world, is seen in this reconstruction as dreamer, naif, do-gooder, bleeding heart, trouble-maker; any or all of the above. (Cf. Jesus for a good example.) Whether the text we wave so piously be the constitution, the Bible, the sacred books of Islam, the Nicene Creed, Marx, Mao, the United Nations Charter, whatever, it all comes down to the same thing: ideals as rhetoric, not to be confused with the real business of living and doing business. Wave the text, by all means, as occasion demands, but don't let the text get in the way of the *real* issues. In this mental gymnastic, ideals are like invested monies: once invested, you don't have to *do* anything about them; they just keep earning dividends. Self-righteousness is the hallmark of idealism as rhetoric, the rallying cry of those who need have no concern about discrepancies between what they profess and what they live. Their self-righteousness, though, is merely cover for the cynicism that really is at the heart of the matter. This mischief, too, each of us is capable of perpetrating.

Given all the mischief we are capable of perpetrating in the name of ideals, would life not be considerably simpler if we forgot all about ideals and concentrated on taking things just as they are, ourselves included? Relax and enjoy life. Go along to get along. Don't rock the boat. This solution is, indeed, alluring. So much so that many settle for it and the contentment it seems to promise. In fact it is the final mischief we can perpetrate, this jettisoning of ideals. The solution is worse than the problem.

We are spirit as well as flesh. The body needs air to breathe and food to eat and water to drink if it is to go on living. No less does the spirit need to breathe and eat and drink if it is not to shrivel up and die within us. "Not by bread alone" remains as true today as when Jesus first said it. One does not feed a hungry body with prayer. Nor does one feed a hungry spirit with a loaf of bread. We may

ignore the needs of the spirit for being just too much
trouble, but that condemns us to spiritual death. We may
put our spirits on a near-starvation diet, but if we do, we
become mean-spirited, incapable of loving ourselves or
anyone else, irrevocably less than all we can be. If we do,
Augustine's restless heart becomes an empty heart, a
hollow heart. Jesus warned us about this when he said,
"You are the salt of the earth. But what if salt becomes
tasteless, what can make it salty again? It is good for
nothing, and can only be thrown out to be trampled un-
derfoot by men" (Mt 5:13–16). Good for nothing. That's
how bluntly the truthful and compassionate Jesus
summed it up.

Jesus left us no way out, really, just as he left himself
no way out. Ideals are undoubtedly part of the cross we
carry—they can complicate, frustrate, drag us down,
wear us out—but we need to be very cautious here,
though. Jesus' story did not end on Calvary. And because
it didn't, Calvary is much more about life than death,
about love than pain. If we are not careful, we can reduce
Jesus' words to a message of gloom and doom, we can
misrepresent the good news so much that it becomes bad
news, indeed—except, perhaps, for masochists and other
self-haters, who see life as nothing more than a death-sen-
tence, and love as nothing more than heartache.

It is easy to forget that the joyous celebration of Easter Sunday is the central celebration of our Christian
faith. *Joy*, that's what we too often leave out of the good
news and out of our faith. Yet, Jesus said he wanted his
joy to be in us, and our joy complete. His very next words,
of course, were these: "This is my commandment: love
one another as I have loved you" (Jn 15:11–12). We have
made so much of the Man of Sorrows, we forget that he
was, far more, a man of joy, and his words a message of
joy. The contemporary artists who have gifted us with
pictures of a smiling, even *laughing* Jesus do much to give

back to Jesus an essential part of his humanity, and give a whole Jesus back to us.

Perhaps we do to joy what we do to inner peace: see it as a gift available to us only when everything is going all right, when there is no struggle or pain. Or is it that we reduce joy to the level of "having fun"? Joy is made of much sterner stuff than that. Joy and struggle, joy and pain are not incompatible. Ask the marathoner who, aching in every muscle, has just successfully completed the race. Ask the mother who holds her newborn infant in her arms for the first time. For that matter, if we have ever loved, we can ask ourselves. Joy goes hand-in-hand with struggle and even, at times, with pain because joy is inseparably linked to love. Joy and inner peace have much to do with one another; so do joy and hope.

Because our faith and our religion are about *serious*, i.e. *important* issues of life and death, have we not allowed faith and religion to become too *serious*, i.e. *dour?* Most of us were taught from our earliest years: you do not laugh in church. Why not? In the world's vast collection of religious art one searches far and wide, and usually in vain, to find a *smiling* face, a happy face. Are frowns easier to paint than smiles? Except for a blessedly enlightened few, most of us have been trapped by our conditioning into believing that there is no place for humor in religion. (Religion, after all, is serious business.) A *laughing* Jesus? A *laughing* God? Yet, how on earth could God have endured us so long unless God had a divinely limitless sense of humor? If we grant the premise and then take another look at creation, we can find evidence of a divine sense of humor peeping out everywhere, not least of all in the way we humans were put together. Perhaps Dante was on to something when he chose to entitle his work, *The Divine Comedy*.

Joy is what brings smiles to faces. A smile spontaneously registers en-joy-ment. Consider when we give someone we love a gift. Is not the best thanks the smile which lights up the face as the loved one sees the gift? Is not the best thanks seeing the loved one *enjoy* the gift, appreciate it—the toy, the sweater, the jewelry? Before we choose the gift we think about the person and what the person likes, needs, enjoys. The smile, the enjoyment tells us we were right. When we don't see this, we conclude we goofed: wrong choice, wrong color, wrong style. (There are some people, of course, whom nothing pleases, but that is another, very sad, story.) Is it too much to suppose that our experience in this images God's? That God wants us to *enjoy* the gifts of life, indeed, that our gratitude for these gifts is best expressed by enjoying them? In fact, we can truly appreciate only what we enjoy, and vice versa.

Our capacity to enjoy, like all our capacities, requires careful development, education, refinement. Enjoyment is yet one more acquired taste. Which parent, caught in the ongoing hassle of "finish what's on your plate first before the dessert" and later the war against junk food, does not know this well? Our capacity to appreciate and enjoy music, architecture, fine literature, film, the sciences, philosophy, to appreciate and enjoy being able to think clearly and understand and express what one thinks—these are the benefits of any education worthy of the name. Indeed, the basic conundrum every teacher faces is the student who demands such enjoyment and appreciation as the *precondition* for taking a course and exerting the necessary effort, when the very purpose of the course is to develop an appreciation and enjoyment that doesn't yet exist; the student who is unwilling to defer gratification.

We live in an era that seems to promise instant-everything: fast-foods, instant photographs, instant communication, instant play-back, instant satisfaction or your money back, instant highs. (All of these are billed as "time-savers." One may well ask: time saved for *what?*) None of this makes the already formidable task of education, a process that cannot be delivered instantly, any easier. Why delay gratification when instant gratification is so readily available? Or so it seems. The major victim of failed education is the failed learner. Cut off from a world of gifts there to be appreciated and enjoyed. A capacity for enjoyment deprived of the opportunity to develop and grow. Mute, inglorious Miltons. Every failed learner is, to a greater or lesser extent, a stranger to joy. But we are all the victims: for every failed learner, there is less joy in the world.

Are not all of us, though, to some extent failed learners? The brilliant scientist, the financial genius, the talented and successful artist, the eloquent preacher who are so driven by their talents that they have never taken the time to learn to enjoy life and the simple gifts of life. "Successful" men and women in every walk of life whose lives are singularly without joy, whose "success" in their walk of life has not made them successful as human beings. In fact every one of us who does not appreciate and enjoy the truly wonderful gifts life bestows so prodigally is a failed learner. In every case the presenting symptom is the same: the absence of joy.

If we are blessed, we are given the opportunity to meet those who *have* learned, whose lives radiate a quiet joy that has little or nothing to do with their life circumstances. They may be rich or poor, in good health or not; they come in all ages, all sizes, all shapes, all colors. Their talents vary, their shortcomings likewise. They may or may not be successful, as we judge such things. None of these traits are what they share in common. They evidence no "profile" of the kind that predictive tests are based on. What they have in common is only (only?!) one thing. They *enjoy* life! They *enjoy* being themselves! Not obtrusively, they have no reason to be obtrusive. Not arrogantly, they are the most live-and-let-live of people. Without a hint of self-congratulation, self-consciousness, self-preoccupation. To encounter their like is like basking in the sun: warming, relaxing, spirit-lifting. Here are the truest teachers who walk the earth, though they'd be the first to scoff at such a preposterous notion. Here are the really holy ones, which notion they'd find even more preposterous. We have much to learn from them. They have learned how to *live*.

Every chapter in this book deals with gifts that life offers us which we fail to appreciate and enjoy, areas of our lives where we are, to a greater or lesser extent, failed learners. Two such gifts we have not yet considered are silence and its inseparable companion, solitude.

Nature provides many sounds, even some noises. Birds chirping, the coyote's howl, claps of thunder, the sounds of rain, the roar of the surf, the whisper of the surf, the whistle of the wind in the trees, for example— but always, if we attend to it carefully, against a background of silence, a silence to which nature returns whenever possible. More than any of the sounds of nature, it is the uncanny silence of nature that speaks to us most loudly. Silence is as necessary to us as sound is. And yet, how many of our waking moments are silent, without sound? For many of us it is the sound of the alarm that pulls us from sleep and begins our day. Quickly to be followed by the sink-side radio, the kitchen radio or TV with morning news, weather reports, talk shows. And as if traffic noises are not enough, there is the radio in the car to protect us from getting too close to silence even in the car. Lest we be exposed to silence in the brief ride in the elevator (heaven forbid!) Muzak is provided. Afoot, the Walkman provides similar relief from silence. And so on through the day, with television waiting for us at the other end. It can be an instructive and very illuminating exercise to count up the minutes (seconds?) of actual silence we experience in the waking hours of our day. It can be even more instructive to note the times when it was *our* deliberate choice, and not the necessity of circumstances beyond our power to control, that precluded silence. For many, silence is virtually unheard of (no pun intended).

The truly wonder-full advances of technology keep finding new and more effective ways, more immediate ways of delivering to us information and entertainment via sensory inputs. When Paul said the eye has not seen, nor the ear heard (1 Cor 2:9), he could just as well have been speaking about the marvels of technology of this age in which we live. The problem is, no one has yet found a way to redesign the human organism and the human psyche to keep up with the developments of technology. These were designed to handle a certain level of inputs per day. Above this level is sensory, mental, and emotional overload. Overload causes stress. Stress generates anxiety. And what do we do about our anxiety? Plug in the earphones, turn on the TV. A vicious cycle that feeds off itself. Much of the stress and anxiety we experience may well be due to nothing more complicated than overload. If so, the remedy is not more inputs but fewer. The remedy is a certain measure of silence (zero external inputs) in our days.

Even while we are the first to complain about "noise pollution"—those external violations of our quiet by others—we remain the principal violators of our own silence. People who can afford to do so buy houses in quiet places, carefully and expensively overseeing the sound-proofing aspects of the construction. Then they proceed to fill the house with the latest and most sophisticated equipment for sound reproduction, often piped throughout the house—their insurance against ever having to tolerate the silence they spent so much money making available. We avoid silence and we have the technology to do it with stunning efficiency. This has been going on for so long, there may well be people-in-the-making for whom silence is a totally alien experience.

One of the main reasons for all of this is silence's

inseparable companion, solitude. To experience silence is to experience solitude. There's the rub. For many solitude is synonymous with loneliness: to be in silence, to be alone, is to be lonely, to feel empty. A young man was asked to imagine himself in his room, alone. Then he was asked, "Is anyone there?" He answered without hesitation: No. That's how he experienced a room in which he was alone: no one was there. *Who is there when we are there all alone?* How sadly many people answer, "No one." They are "no one" to themselves, strangers to themselves. As it was for that young man, a room with only them in it is, for them, an empty room. What does this say about their connectedness with themselves? What does this say about their connectedness with the in-dwelling God?

It is only in silence and solitude that we are able to hear the inner voices which tell us there is someone in there, that we are not a "no one." But if lonely feelings so frighten us that we cannot bear to be alone, to be silent, we never give ourselves the chance to hear those inner voices, to listen to all they have to tell us. We never give ourselves the chance to learn that solitude is not synonymous with loneliness, that solitude can be a deeply enriching experience, offering us the opportunity to encounter and come to know something more about ourselves.

We have been conditioned to think that loneliness is an affliction that only others and their company can relieve us of—a spouse, a friend, drinking buddies, bridge partners. According to this way of thinking, any lonely feelings are a sure indication that these others have failed us. According to this way of thinking, when we finally have enough "right" others, loneliness will be banished forever from our lives. Then how do we explain that some of our most poignant and painful experiences of loneliness occur precisely when we are in the midst of the "right" others, even dearly loved others? As one person put it: "It is far easier for me to bear being alone when I'm by myself than when I am in the midst of others." Could it be that loneliness is only secondarily related to others and the company of others, that the primary reason for loneliness is our lack of a satisfactory relationship with our *selves?* our lack of self-knowledge, self-possession? Silence and solitude are prerequisite for encountering our selves. Without such encounters we can never truly make friends with ourselves.

When we remember that the voice of God's Holy Spirit is among the inner voices waiting to catch our ear, we can see why silence and solitude are essential for encountering the God within us, for allowing God to encounter us. The open heart is the listening heart, the open mind, the listening mind. We need silence to do that, and solitude.

Which is why the life of the spirit needs silence and solitude. We do well to make friends with them.

If we are ever to make friends with holiness, we first have to let go of our definitions of holiness. We have to remove from holiness the medieval robes in which we have clothed it, the frown on its face, the rippling muscles (spiritual, of course), the ethereal halo around its head. Then what *does* holiness look like, what face does it wear? Just look in the mirror. To which most of us respond, "Who, *me?!*" That's what we've done to holiness—made it into something for someone else, surely not *us*. Priests, ministers, and religious, holiness is their business. Those human beings who show up once in a blue moon—we call them saints—holiness is their business. We are just ordinary human beings, trying to get by, trying (barely) to make ends meet (spiritual as well as material). What does holiness have to do with us? Everything, if Jesus can be believed.

We are God's holy people because God dwells in us, God's love dwells in us. We are holy every time we let God's love have its say in us: every time we choose forgiveness over revenge; every time we choose to take our hands out of our pockets and help someone in need, even though our hands hold very little; every time we choose trust over self-protection, peace over strife, love over hate. We are holy every time we let God's love shine on us, and through us. So ordinary. So down-to-earth. So simple. Why, even *we* can be holy sometimes!

Jesus, who was not given to exaggeration, much less to tampering with the truth, addressed this remarkable invitation, not just to anyone, but to those who were struggling and felt it was all just too much: "Come to me, all you who labor and are overburdened, and I will give you rest. Shoulder my yoke and learn from me, for I am gentle and humble in heart, and you will find rest for your souls. Yes, my yoke is easy and my burden light" (Mt 11:28–30).

Life, by any sane reckoning, is not a bed of roses. Following Jesus inevitably takes us by Calvary. But consider this: are any of the alternatives easier? It is easier to have faith and trust than it is to bear the crushing burden of despair and cynicism. It is easier to love, for all the pain of it, than it is to bear the corrosive burden of hate. It is easier to walk in the light of truth, with all the frightful sights that offend our eyes and wound our hearts in its glare, than it is to wrestle with the ghosts of the dark.

As to the restlessness all this consigns us to, Jesus promised us that we would find rest for our souls. That, coming from Jesus, is no small promise.

In all of this we simply cannot afford to be failed learners. There is far too much at stake.

There's a Place

High in the mountains where there's snow
There's a place, I know! I know!
Where all is crystal air and bright,

Where shadows fade and all is light.
High in the mountains where there's snow.

Deep in the forests where trees grow
There's a place, I know! I know!
Where all is leafy fern and calm.
Where troubles end and all is balm.
Deep in the forests where trees grow.

Far over oceans where winds blow
There's a place, I know! I know!
Where all is dappled sun and fair.
Where sorrows end without a care.
Far over oceans where winds blow.

Here in my heart where silence swells
Is there a place where all this dwells?
Here in my heart where I'm alone
Is there a place that's all my own?
Why in the mountains? Why in the sea?
There's no such place, if it's not in me.

High in the mountains where there's snow
There's a place, I know! I know!

7. Making Friends with Good Enough

*"This treasure we possess in earthen vessels to
make it clear that its surpassing power comes
from God and not from us" (2 Cor 4:7).*

Some of our deepest truths emerge from the stories
we tell about ourselves. Stories have a way of doing that.
But as long as these stories we read and hear remain for
us merely stories about somebody else, they can tell us
little or nothing about ourselves. Unless we find our own
stories, thinly disguised, in these stories handed on to us
by others, we can go on thinking that our stories have
never been told before, which is only a small part of the
truth. In addition to our own limited store of experience,
we have the accumulated experience of those who have
gone before us, there for us to draw on if we know where to
find it, if we know how to recognize it once we do find it.

Many tales in religious literature have as their theme
the person who sets out to search the world over for the
grail, the treasure, the truth, only to return home empty-
handed—to find it in his own backyard. The point of these
tales is not that all the searching was totally wasted effort. It was, after all, only by the searching far and wide
that the person was able finally to recognize and appreciate what lay in his own backyard, in her own heart. How
much of our stories can we find and recognize here?

We might begin by considering all that we so mindlessly call "ordinary" in our lives, all that we take for
granted. Ordinary as in ho-hum. Ordinary as in scarcely
worthy of our careful attention, much less our love. Ordinary as in disposable, readily replaceable, unextraordi-

nary. This "ordinary" is an adult human word. There is no such word in the vocabulary of God, for whom all that is falls within the loving embrace of God's closest attention, care, and love. "Look at the birds in the sky. They do not sow or reap or gather into barns; yet your heavenly Father feeds them. . . . Think of the flowers growing in the fields; they never have to work or spin; yet I assure you that not even Solomon in all his regalia was robed like one of these" (Mt 6:26,28–29). What could be more ordinary than birds, than wildflowers growing everywhere? Not so in God's eyes.

Nor is "ordinary" in a little child's vocabulary. Such a child hasn't had enough time or education yet to have lost the sense of wonder. A child is still enthralled by the sheer newness of everything, still asking a hundred why's, still capable of amazement at the way a spider spins a web, a flower has petals that come off if you pull on them, paper tears, and things make a funny noise when you drop them. For a child nothing is ordinary, unexceptional. Was Jesus alluding to this not-yet-lost sense of wonder when he named the child as the primary candidate for the kingdom of God? ". . . for it is to such as these that the kingdom of God belongs. I tell you solemnly, anyone who does not welcome the kingdom of God like a little child will never enter it" (Mk 10:14–15).

We learn so quickly to dismiss the ordinary and to over-value the extraordinary in our lives. Are not special holidays and other extraordinary events so often a let-down and a disappointment because we make too much of them, expect too much of them? By the same token, we undervalue the everyday blessings in our lives, as if the very largesse that lets them be ours not just once in a while but every day is to be reckoned a disfavor to us. Is it our need for diversion, for excitement? Or that we so easily fall prey to boredom? Our response to things is determined by the way we perceive them. Not only beauty is in the eye of the beholder. So is ordinariness. But how

quickly the scales fall from our eyes when we are threatened with the loss of what we so facilely dismiss as
ordinary!

Do we know how truly wonderful it is to be alive? We
would if we were faced with a life-threatening illness. How
wonderful it is to have a roof over our heads and food on
the table? We would if we were about to become part of the
homeless and the hungry. How wonderful to be able to see
and hear? We would if we were threatened with blindness
or deafness. All of this we call ordinary and take for
granted.

We don't have to wait until we are threatened with its
loss to appreciate what we have. We can take time out
actually to look at all that we call ordinary in our lives,
and then try to imagine what our lives would be like without these. Does it all still seem quite so "ordinary" to us?

It was the very ordinariness of Jesus that blinded
many to who he really was. Joseph, the carpenter's son.
Mary's son. (Wasn't there some scandal about those
two?) Native of Galilee by way of Nazareth. The familiar of
shepherds and sheep, reaping and sowing, children's
games and wedding feasts, the care of vineyards, the way
yeast works—all the down-to-earth, simple and, yes, ordinary ingredients of every human life. His familiarity with
the ordinary, though, did not breed contempt, for he saw
the hand of God in all things. Paradoxically, it was the
very ordinariness of Jesus that has made him one of us
and ours forever, and we, his. He can plead for us ordinary
mortals at the right hand of the Father because he well
knows what it is to be an ordinary mortal, like us. This is
the true wonder and glory of this man of Nazareth
through whom God came to dwell in our midst and in us.

When we see with the eyes of faith, nothing is only
what it seems to be, least of all the ordinary.

We build cathedrals and temples, mosques and
shrines. We raise monuments to our faith in God, houses
of God. And it is good that we do this. We need tangible

ways to give expression to our faith, tangible reminders of
our faith. Done with art and care, the simplest of these
can truly lift the mind and heart to God, the most magnificent are invitations to a transcendent experience. For all
these reasons, such places are sacred to us, our holy
places. But herein lies a problem.

As soon as we designate some places as holy, as
sacred, we inevitably, howsoever implicitly, designate
other places as neither holy nor sacred. The sacred and
the profane. Whatever philosophical and theological
merit there may be in distinguishing one from the other,
what we *do* in practice with this differentiation does violence to the truth. It is God's indwelling presence, and
that alone, which constitutes the holy and the sacred.
And God happens to be everywhere, in all that is. The
Holy Spirit still breathes wherever the wind of God's love
takes it, wherever our love for one another takes it. Is God
any less present in a kindergarten, a business office, a
family room, the local bus, the shopping center—any of
the places where the necessities of our lives take us? God
is present in defeat no less than in victory, in heartache
no less than in ecstasy, in the darkest night no less than
high noon. God is everywhere. The question is: do we *see*
that God is everywhere? recognize God's holy presence in
all that is?

Reverence is the human response to what we perceive
as sacred. Do we truly reverence all the goodness that is
around us and in us—flawed goodness, of course, but
goodness nonetheless? Do we reverence life and what is
genuinely life-giving? At the very least, reverence requires of us that we treat what is sacred with respect. Do
we treat the gift of life with respect? Do we treat our
environment with respect? Do we treat ourselves and one
another with respect? The danger in designating only
some things, some places, some people as sacred is that it
gives us license to treat the rest with disrespect, disre-
garding what is, after all, merely profane. In the light of

faith, this is the ultimate profanity. God observes no such differentiation.

Nor did Jesus, the only Son of the Father. Yes, it is true that Jesus drove the buyers and sellers out of the temple in Jerusalem, quoting scripture, ". . . my house will be called a house of prayer, but you are turning it into a thieves' den" (Mt 21:13–14). But Jesus also said to the Samaritan woman by that well: "Believe me, woman, the hour is coming when you will worship the Father neither on this mountain nor in Jerusalem. . . . But the hour will come—in fact it is already here—when true worshipers will worship the Father in spirit and truth" (Jn 4:21–23).

The real profanation against which Jesus inveighed was thievery, regardless of where it takes place. Jesus' parables are filled with his reverence for all of life and the manifestations of life. Even, incredibly, for his enemies. The accounts of his interactions with whomever, whatever, he met consistently manifest his reverence for the goodness, howsoever struggling for life, he found in others, and his respect for what he found. His reverence went far beyond respect. Jesus *loved* what he found, and in loving it, healed it. In fact Jesus' whole life taught us this: love, and love alone, removes the scales from our eyes and permits us to see the sacredness in all that is, and seeing it, reverence it.

Nowhere is this more difficult to learn than when it comes to ourselves. Psychology can teach us much about the necessity of *accepting* our here-and-now, wounded selves as the first step in growing toward wholeness, but only our faith can bring us to see that mere acceptance is not a response of faith, only reverence is. Our faith calls us to *reverence* ourselves, to see ourselves as sacred, to treat ourselves with respect. The core evil of sin, and that which makes it so offensive to the God who loves us, is the profound disrespect for ourselves that every sin entails.

We are conditioned from our earliest years to watch

out for self-love, selfishness, self-seeking, as if these were tigers waiting behind every bush to leap out and gobble us up. The net result of this conditioning leaves us distrusting ourselves, on constant guard against ourselves, treating ourselves as the enemy. It is sadly, even tragically ironic that we should be warned so assiduously about the dangers of loving ourselves too much, when the lifelong, painfully hard-fought struggle for each of us is learning to love ourselves nearly enough.

No small part of the problem is a confusion of language. Consider this passage from Matthew's gospel (Mt 16:24–28): "If a man wishes to come after me, he must deny his very self, take up his cross, and begin to follow in my footsteps. Whoever would save his life will lose it, but whoever loses his life for my sake will find it. What profit would a man show if he were to gain the whole world and destroy himself in the process? What can a man offer in exchange for his very self?" In one and the same passage Jesus seems to refer to the denial of self as a condition for following him, and then describes the self as something so precious that not even gaining the whole world could compensate for its destruction. How do we make sense of this?

The ambiguity and confusion stem mainly from the failure to differentiate between what, in contemporary language, we have come to call the *ego* and the *self*. The ego is the executive dimension of the psyche, the aspect that oversees getting things done. The arena over which the ego presides involves doing, action: organizing, planning, striving, accomplishing, competing. The ego is, obviously, a necessary and important part of the psyche. It can, when tempered, accomplish wonders. But the ego is notoriously prone to being carried away. The thrill of accomplishment tips us so easily into success at any price. The kudos that go to the winner are a heady wine we can all too easily become addicted to, so that winning becomes everything. The heat and challenge of competition too readily cast the competitor in the role of enemy, to be defeated. Power fuels the ego.

Self is the contemporary term roughly equivalent to spirit or soul. Whereas *doing* is the arena in which ego functions, *being* is the arena of the self. Presence, sharing, giving—these are functions of the self. So is play. So are love and friendship. To the extent that ego intrudes in these, there is competition, manipulation, a contest rather than sharing, a negotiation rather than giving. Love, not power, fuels the self.

Perhaps an example best shows the difference. A man arrives at his office and, from nine to five, does what he has been hired to do. He gets done what needs to be gotten done that day, attends and contributes to organizational and planning meetings, meets with potential customers, makes decisions and sees to their implementation. This is all largely ego-function. After dinner that evening he takes time out to be with his three year old son. He holds him, plays a game with him, reads him a story. He isn't accomplishing anything; he is simply being with his son, loving his son. This is the self functioning.

In our society ego is all but idolized; self is scarcely understood, is the object of suspicion, distrust, derision. Achievement is the sole measure of success. And so accomplishment becomes the sole basis for self-esteem. (At least here—*self*-esteem, not *ego*-esteem—the language has it right, though in the wrong context.) Pulled by our society, we become so busy and caught up in doing, there is no time just to be; in fact we barely even know what that means. Ego says: what I *do* is all that is important. Self says: what I *am* is all important, which takes no small courage and faith. Our society bestows all its awards and rewards on what we do, scarcely pausing long enough even to notice what we are.

The point is not that what we do is unimportant and

of no consequence. Of course it is. The point is that *why* we do it and *how* we do it makes the difference between following in the footsteps of Jesus and selling our souls, our selves.

In Matthew's passage Jesus is telling us that his followers have to renounce unbridled *ego*, not self. We have to renounce power and the blinding ambition, the driving ambition that power's corrupting influence invariably generates. Jesus turned his back on power and the uses of power. "Egotistical" says it far more accurately, less ambiguously, than "selfish." Ego, for all the adulation it receives (and craves), is the real culprit. Self is the first of ego's victims. Jesus made it clear where he stood regarding the self: not even winning the whole world can compensate for the destruction or ruin of self.

Might these parables also tell us something about the value God places on ourselves? "The kingdom of heaven is like a treasure hidden in a field which someone has found; he hides it again, goes off happy, sells everything he has and buys the field. Again, the kingdom of heaven is like a merchant looking for fine pearls; when he finds one of great value he goes and sells everything he owns and buys it" (Mt 13:44–46). The kingdom of heaven, after all, is within us—*is* us.

Perhaps love's most terrifying aspect is this: love is the giving of *self*. Not money, not things, not accomplishments, not success, not any of the prizes ego can gain for us, though the sharing of these may express love. Without the gift of self, though, all this other giving is no more than an attempt to buy the one thing that absolutely cannot be bought: another's love. Terrifying because the self, for most of us, remains so dubiously desirable a gift to bestow (wrong size? wrong color? wrong style?). Unlike other gifts there is no taking this one back to exchange for something more appealing. Love happens between selves or, whatever the appearances, it is not love. Ego is the intruder here. Unless there is some measure of self-esteem, self-possession, however tenuous, love cannot happen.

Self-possession is another of those happily-on-the-target expressions that has volumes to tell us if we pay close enough attention to it. Each of us begins life with a clear, God-given title to the self that is to emerge from within us. It belongs to us; we are given exclusive ownership rights and responsibilities. But long before the self has even had the chance to stand on its own two wobbly feet, all kinds of liens against the property, shares in the property bought and paid for, rights-of-way through the property have been established by others. The question of who owns what and who is responsible for what becomes the subject of most of the disputes that strew our path toward independence and the beginnings of adulthood—and beyond. Perhaps as good a way as any of describing human growth toward wholeness is this: it is the process of clearing title to one's self. An adult, then, is one who exercises exclusive ownership rights and responsibilities for oneself. The self may be freely shared, but there is no question of either ownership or responsibility: adults own and take responsibility for themselves. In a word, an adult is *self-possessed*. For most of us the process of clearing the title takes a lifetime.

There is a corollary to all of this. With the exception of parents of young children and those charged with the care of others who are incapable of taking care of themselves, all of us are responsible *only* for ourselves. We are not responsible for anyone else. We are responsible *to* others, but there is a world of difference between being responsible *for* and responsible *to* someone. We are responsible to others in many ways. Treating others with the respect that is their due. Honoring agreements and keeping promises that we make to others. Helping others out in their need when we have the means to help. These are a few of the ways we are responsible *to* others. But we cannot live anyone else's life for that person. We cannot make another's decisions for that person. We cannot relieve anyone of the burden of responsibility each of us must carry for ourselves. With what pain caring parents come to see and finally accept this! How painfully anyone who loves and cares about somebody else comes to see and accept this! Every helping professional either recognizes this or perishes in the attempt to do the impossible.

Hidden in the nooks and crannies of these reflections, and allegedly what this chapter is all about, is the concept of "good enough." It is time to bring it out in the open. Somewhere toward the middle of that grading scale which has mediocrity, or worse, at one extreme and perfection at the other lies "good enough." This zone of the scale is where, with God's grace, we live and move and have our being. The perfectionist's scale has no such zone: there is nothing between perfection and mediocrity. How, one wonders, does the perfectionist grade Michelangelo's *David,* Shakespeare's *Hamlet,* Beethoven's *Fifth Symphony,* mother's chocolate cake? None of them perfect; are they, for that reason, to be considered mediocrities? The notion is patently ridiculous when we apply it to works of art, but what about ourselves and our own lives?

What an inestimable grace it is to recognize and appreciate all that is good enough in ourselves and in our lives! Good enough for our love, our loyalty, our dedication. Good enough to give ourselves to it wholeheartedly and single-mindedly. Good enough to merit our humble gratitude. Good enough does not close the door on improvement or growth, does not deny the possibility of more. Perhaps good enough *for now* says it more accurately. Good enough insists there is something between perfection and mediocrity.

Parents who had their full share of shortcomings, who easily made their allotted quota of mistakes. Parents who had their own task of growing up to attend to, even as they tended to their children's. Parents who had ups and downs in their own relationship with each other. But parents who loved their children and tried to do their best by them, according to their own lights. Parents who were there when needed, willing to give what they had to give. *Good enough* parents. Not the best, but good enough.

A college of medium size and financial resources, with a reasonably competent and responsible administration. A college whose physical facilities were adequate—library, gym, playing fields, cafeteria—but with few frills and even fewer luxuries. A college which offered a fairly solid basic curriculum in the traditional majors, but somewhat thin on the number of electives and specialized courses. A college whose faculty was probably about par for the course: a number of so-so teachers, some duds, and a few truly gifted teachers. A college whose student body provided the opportunity to encounter a varied cross-section of one's peers. *Good enough* education. Not the best, but good enough.

A life that has its share of successes and failures, smiles and tears, long-stretching plateaus. A life that has its deserts and its oases. A life blessed with friends and acquaintances who are a somewhat mixed lot, bedeviled by enemies at some points. A life enriched by gains, wounded by losses. A life of faith, sometimes seeing, sometimes not seeing, but always trying to trust God. A life with God manifestly in it at times, but at other times seemingly far away, absent. A *good enough* life. Not the best, but good enough.

Though the details differ, can we not, if we look honestly, find so very much in our own lives that is good enough? So very much in ourselves, thanks to God's grace, that is good enough? We cheat ourselves of much hard-earned tranquillity if we allow the ordinariness of it all (no small part of its gift) to blind us to the wonderful blessings of what is good enough. For now.

One of the many gifts nature bestows on us is that

nature allows us, without our even noticing it, to suspend our critical faculties and to see with an uncritical eye. "That mountain over there should be slightly farther east and not so craggy." "There should be more red and a little less yellow in those clouds catching the setting sun." "That oak tree is too gnarly and its branches are too twisted." Even to imagine saying such things shows them to be ridiculous, not to say grotesque. Nature inspires in us an awe that makes such thoughts unthinkable. We don't have to *try* not to think them; we just don't. Nature beguiles us into letting things be just as they are and speak for themselves. And so nature touches the mind and heart and soul in ways that nothing else can in quite the same way. It is the despair of artists, even the most successful, that they cannot capture *all* of it.

We are part of God's creation, a part of nature. If we could only learn to set aside our critical faculties and see ourselves with an uncritical eye. There is so much there to see that goes unseen! If we could only learn to allow what is there in us to speak for itself. There is so much there that goes unsaid—voices crying in the wilderness of our misunderstood hearts. Misunderstood, not merely by others, but by us. A single, uncritical glimpse of ourselves as God sees us would transform us. In the beatific vision, we have been promised, we will see God face-to-face for the first time. We will also be seeing ourselves face-to-face for the first time. We needn't wait till then, really, to see God; we needn't wait till then to see ourselves.

Each of us has been given a garden to grow. Plants of all kinds, some of them bearing flowers and fruit. Some of the fruit is edible, some not. Some of the flowers bloom only for a day, others for much longer. Some of the trees lose their leaves, others do not. All of them need tending. Some of the tending nature provides, some we have to provide. Watering. Fertilizing. Trimming back. Each plant has its own peculiarities, requires its own care. As in any garden, weeds grow. Our tendency is to go after the weeds as soon as they appear and root them out. Jesus cautioned us against doing this (Mt 13:24-30). The reason for the caution is most instructive: we are not very good at telling the difference between what is weed and what isn't. We could be pulling up the flowers without knowing it. Better to let things grow until the difference is unmistakable. With growing things, when they're beginning and fragile and just finding their way, you can't tell the difference between weeds and the rest.

In God's kingdom we are growing things, just beginning, fragile, finding our way. We need to be very careful about what we call weeds in our garden.

The analogy thus far is incomplete, if our faith is to have a place in it. While we have been given a share in tending our garden, the Holy Spirit is the head gardener. We neither select the plants nor make them grow. We can only allow them to grow, each in its own time and way, by our care. It is up to us, with God's help, to come to know and appreciate the garden we have been given. We are asked not to compare it to other gardens because each garden is different and there are more plants than can fit in any one garden. We are asked to respect the authority of the head gardener and trust his superior knowledge of gardens and growing things—and fledgling gardeners.

Once again, true wisdom is seeing as God sees. This is especially important to remember when it comes to judging ourselves and our lives. Our judgments are so skewed that good enough gets lost in the shuffle; flowers are mistaken for weeds. Overly harsh, impatient, lacking in compassion, intolerant, and ultimately lacking even in understanding, our judgments make less of ourselves than we are; our judgments so focus on what is not there that we fail to appreciate all that *is* there. This is our failing, not God's. This is not how God judges us.

God is not a perfectionist. (Not even heaven could help us if God were!) God's providential care embraces all that is. The loving, compassionate Father revealed by

Jesus (like Father, like Son) loves life down to its merest whispers, sustains and cherishes life in all its forms, waits patiently for seeds to sprout, nestlings to fly, buds to respond to the sun and burst into bloom. Just as God waits patiently as we open our minds and our hearts to the Holy Spirit. Never all at once. Never completely. Never once and for all. That's all right with God. Is it all right with us? To assume that our judgments of ourselves reflect God's judgment of us is presumptuous beyond belief. Beyond belief in God and who God is.

John told us who God is: God is love (1 Jn 4:8). On the other hand, Paul gave us a description of love that has rung true for the centuries that separate Paul from us (1 Cor 13). If John was right, do we not have in Paul's thirteenth chapter a description of God? Listen:

God is always patient and kind; God is never jealous; God is never boastful or conceited; God is never rude or selfish; God does not take offense, and is not resentful. God takes no pleasure in other people's sins but delights in the truth; God is always ready to excuse, to trust, to hope, and to endure whatever comes. God does not come to an end . . .

Is it not safe to leave judgment of ourselves and our lives in the hands of such a God? Is this not good enough for us? For now?

A Modern Parable

Jesus went walking in Rome one day. You couldn't see him, of course, because he had fairly given up making appearances on earth until his final return. He roamed aimlessly, letting his feet take him where they would, the way you do when you're just out walking.

And on his walk that day Jesus saw many people and many things, as one does on such walks. But only three stayed in his mind.

That night his Father asked him, "Did you enjoy your walk today, my son?"

And Jesus answered, "Oh, yes, Papa."

"Did you see anything interesting?" his Father asked.

And Jesus answered, "Three times I saw myself in Rome."

"Did you now, my son. Tell me about it."

"The first time was just off St. Peter's Square. There I saw this ancient, bearded rabbi walking along with his hands behind his back, muttering to himself. He was in such anguish for his people! The second time was by the Spanish Steps. Understand me when I say this, Papa. A child, really, he was there picking pockets—and doing so quite successfully! He is a child of the streets, Papa. And the third time, I can't remember just where it was, this woman with a child in each hand. She's divorced, Papa, and struggles to love her children without the help of their father.

And his Father said, with a sigh, "When will you ever learn, my son?"

And Jesus said, "But I did learn, Papa."

His Father said, "Did I not send you to earth, my only son, to tell them about my goodness and love?"

"Yes, Papa, and I did. But I also listened, and they told me about their pain."

"Is not their pain of their own choosing, my son?" his Father asked him.

Then Jesus said, "Pain, wherever it comes from, is pain, Papa."

Sternly now, his Father said, "My son, you let your human heart carry you away."

"Yes, Papa, I did," Jesus whispered.

Then his Father smiled and reached out and embraced his son, happy that he had sent his son, happy that his son went walking in Rome that day.

8. Making Friends with Death

"I tell you most solemnly, unless a grain of wheat falls on the ground and dies, it remains only a single grain; but if it dies, it yields a rich harvest" (Jn 12:24).

There is no way, much as we wish it, that we can get to Easter Sunday without passing through Good Friday. While Good Friday is not the end of Jesus' story, it is a chapter that cannot be skipped without losing the whole point of the story. Life, in every form that we experience it, is inseparably intertwined with death, so imperceptibly a part of nature and nature's cycles that we pay it little attention, scarcely notice it. We do not think of an oak tree as an acorn that used to be, nor a hawk soaring in the sky as an egg that ceased to be. In a million ways death and new life and death are going on all around us. Beginnings and endings and yet new beginnings.

When death with its awful finality touches our lives in the dying of those we love, we experience the terrible anguish of loss, the soul-searing grief of irrevocable separation, wounds that all of time never fully heal. And our own death? The very thought of this summons forth all our nightmare demons and unthinkable terrors, all disasters rolled into one: pain we don't even want to think about; the ultimate loss of control, loss of ourselves we don't want to think about; a final, brutal probing of our fragile faith that doesn't bear thinking about. Our own death? Unthinkable.

So, naturally, we want to think about death as little as possible. We want to hide from death, as if, hiding, we can make it harder for death to find us. We want to deny death. We try euphemisms: passing on, expiring, falling asleep. We try to disguise it in other ways, as so many of our funeral customs do. We try to disguise it as just one more disease that medicine, given time, will find the cure for, as it has done for so many other diseases. We try to hide it by disguising—cosmetically, surgically, chemically—the aging process that reminds us of death, that leads us to death. We pretend that death isn't real; if we don't talk about it, it will just go away; if we cover its face (or ours), it will disappear.

But there are good and holy reasons for us to think about death, to give it a place in our conscious awareness of life. The first and most obvious is that death, including our own, is simply a fact of life, a given: it is appointed to each of us once to die. It is good and holy for us to think about the facts of our lives, especially the unpleasant facts. The more these are given a place in our conscious awareness, are out in the open, the more available they are to the light of God's grace, the touch of God's love. The more these are shut away in the dark and ignored, the more liable they are to work their mischief on us, unchecked. There are those who argue, rather convincingly, that our attempts to ignore and deny death have much to do with the anxiety that lies under and fuels all our other anxieties.

While there are good and holy reasons to think about death, there are also bad and unholy reasons for doing so. Fire-and-brimstone, death-and-destruction sermons, contrived to strike terror into the heart, are a form of spiritual blackmail. Engender enough fear, make the threat serious enough, and people will do anything—for a while. Fear is the key word. There are ways of thinking about death that do no more than play on our fears, that generate morbid and depressing thoughts, or generate a kind of hysterical piety. If these were the only reasons for thinking about death, we would be better off banishing it from our thoughts. But there are better reasons than these for giving death a space in our conscious awareness.

We make more choices than we realize about what we allow space for in our conscious awareness and how much space we give it. This, to a large extent, determines what we pay attention to, how we read our environment, what we are sensitive and responsive to. An architect notices much more about the buildings he passes on the street than the rest of us; he is much more aware of structural realities than we are. After all, it's his business. So does a landscape artist notice plants; a politician, poll results; a clothes designer, clothes. For most of us work, and what affects our working situation, is given a large space in our awareness. Family is also, and friends. The process is selective: we *choose* what we will give space to and how much. There simply isn't room for everything, so we *have* to choose. Obviously, we give space to what we consider important and pass over what we consider of little or no importance to us. Which of us, for instance, spends much time thinking about the life-span of the flea or what actually happens to guitar strings after they break? We don't. We would, though, if it were important to us. In fact the contents of conscious awareness are a good indicator of what we consider important in our lives.

Consciousness raising is the name we have given to the process of giving space in our conscious awareness to what had no space before, or giving a larger space to what had very little space before. Racism. Sexism. The plight of the hungry and the homeless. The environment. The fragile oneness of planet earth. Though we still have an immense way to go, we are becoming increasingly aware of these issues, pay more attention to them, are more sensitive to them than we were in the past. We are more aware because we have given them more space in our conscious awareness.

How much space do we give God and our faith in our consciousness? There are those who give none or next to

none; their faith consequently has little to do with the
realities of their lives. Others have made such a space for
faith and God that these are as much a part of their everyday lives as the sun's rising, the coming of night. For
most of us there is plenty of room for consciousness raising when it comes to God's place in our lives. But the
choice is up to us. How much do we want God and our
faith to have a place in our conscious lives? If we want
God to have more space, we're back to consciousness
raising. And death. Awareness of death can profoundly
raise our consciousness of God and faith, our consciousness of who we are and what we're here for.

We say of persons whose deaths are more or less im-
minent that they are living on borrowed time. But when
we allow ourselves to think about our own dying, is it not
clear that every one of us is living on borrowed time? Life
is a gift entrusted to us for a time; then God will ask us to
give it back. Remembering this helps us appreciate how
wonderful a gift time is, how precious each day is. Consciously acknowledging that life is a gift to be returned
keeps before our minds the purpose for which the gift was
given to us: to love God, to love one another. It is only in
the light of this purpose that we can know what is truly
important in life and what isn't. Surely this will be clear to
us finally when we come to our dying. But we don't have to
wait until then, when it is too late to do anything about it,
to know what is important and what isn't. If we give our
dying a conscious place in our living, we can know now,
while there is still time to do something about it.

Perspective on our lives is what awareness of death
has to give us. Thinking about death is good and holy, not
so much for what it teaches us about dying, but for what it
can teach us about living. We can learn to ask ourselves,
"How, looking back from my deathbed, would I have
wanted myself to decide and choose in this situation
which confronts me now?" Asking the question this way
shows us that the only really important question always

is, one way or another: what is the most loving thing to do in these circumstances? That is, after all, why we are here on earth. And, all too often, it is the very last question that occurs to us to ask ourselves.

Perspective on control is what awareness of death has to give us. Like so many words in our language, control is made to bear too heavy a burden for one word. Control bespeaks so much that is good and necessary. Being in control enables us to live and function as rational (more or less) human beings. Being out of control is irrational and dangerous. The right to control our own lives, make our own decisions, chart our own course is the essence of the freedom our democratic form of government was established to preserve. For all its failings and abuses, its *de facto* constraints on that freedom, economic and otherwise, our country stands out in a world of tyrannies, large and small, governments which judge it best that such freedoms are not for the good of the country or its people. Being in control as opposed to helplessness. Control as synonymous with competency, efficiency, getting the job done. Control as acceptance of one's own responsibility for oneself. Control as ego-restraint. All good and necessary. As far as it goes.

And here is where the problem with control lies, the vice that can be spawned by the virtue. For all the loveliness of being in control, the truth is that there is much that is beyond our power to control, much that is beyond our right to control. Topping the list: we cannot add a single day to our given lifespan. We can do much that shortens that span, even brings it to an end, but we do not have the power to lengthen it beyond its allotted time. If we can face and accept that one, the rest become progressively easier. We can exercise a certain measure of control over our inputs—our care, our planning, our hard work, our love—but we cannot control the outcomes. These depend on so much that is beyond our power to control. We have no control over the responses of others to us, nor do we have any right to try to exercise control there. We cannot control events. We cannot *make* anything happen (all appearances to the contrary notwithstanding); we can only allow it to happen and then choose our response to what happens or doesn't. What grief and frustration and wasted effort we can spare ourselves and others when we let go the delusion that we are in control of everything and everything depends on us!

We end the Lord's Prayer with these words: "For the kingdom, the power, and the glory are yours, now and forever." We say the prayer so often the words become rote. We would do well to pause and listen to what we are acknowledging in this prayer. This is still God's kingdom, not ours. Though one hardly gets that impression from the mass media, God still presides over the universe and all that is in it, God has relinquished not one iota of divine power or divine responsibility. We are asked to surrender that which we cannot control, not into other hands as inept as ours, but into God's hands. The expression "out of control" in this context, because incomplete, is misleading. We are asked to be out of *our* control so that we can be in *God's* control. Which, considering the relative competencies, isn't such a bad deal. In that ultimate out-of-control experience which is death, it will be into God's hands that we surrender control.

Perspective on security is another gift that awareness of death has to offer us. And, as with the word control, security speaks out of both sides of its mouth. A basic security as to life's necessities—enough food on the table, a roof over one's head—is good and surely intended for all of us by our munificent creator. A person who has to wonder where the next meal is coming from or how to find shelter from the night's cold is hardly free to give attention to other human concerns. (Is not one of the continuing shameful evils in our society—a sin that surely cries to heaven for vengeance—the existence in our opulent midst of so many who, through no fault of their own, are denied the basic necessities of life?) A basic security about walking down the street without having to fear getting mugged or raped, about the sanctity of one's home, about the right to work for one's living and receive just compensation—these are certainly reasonable desires that all of us have. No one lives on love and pale moonlight. Being able to count on a certain stability in our lives so that everything isn't up for grabs every time we turn around. A legitimate expectation that one can have is planning and providing for future needs, future contingencies, so that one need not fear becoming a burden on others—these also fall within a reasonable exercise of our responsibility for taking care of ourselves. Regardless of the circumstances which may prevent us from enjoying any of these securities in our lives, our *wanting* them cannot be faulted. What can be faulted, and was denounced by Jesus, was an excessive, obsessive preoccupation with building a security that is bullet-proof, future-proof, life-proof, and ultimately God-proof.

The question is what comes *first* for us in the crunch. Is God and God's word a luxury we can indulge only after we have seen to our securities? Is our faith something to be trotted out only when the real business of living has been taken care of, like a cherished hobby—collecting rare coins, refurbishing old cars? one more achievement award? This isn't what Jesus taught.

"O weak in faith! Stop worrying, then, over questions like 'What are we to eat?' or 'What are we to drink?' or 'What are we to wear?' The unbelievers are always running after these things. Your heavenly Father knows all that you need. Seek first his kingship over you, his way of holiness, and all these things will be given you besides. Enough, then, of worry about tomorrow. Let tomorrow take care of itself. Today has troubles enough of its own" (Mt 6:30–34).

The gospel (like death) calls us to a radical insecurity that cuts across a comfortable bank balance, a paid-up life insurance policy, a retirement fund. On the one hand, the gospel does not exempt us from the effort to provide reasonably for ourselves. On the other, the gospel constantly reminds us that there are other values more important than security, that life itself involves risk, carries no built-in guarantees, none. What the gospel holds out to us as truly life-giving and spirit-filling is not security but *trust* in God's providential love for us. "Are not two sparrows sold for next to nothing? Yet not a single sparrow falls to the ground without your Father's consent. As for you, every hair of your head has been counted: so do not be afraid of anything. You are worth more than an entire flock of sparrows" (Mt 10:28–31). Trust in God's love, trust in our own worth, this is what heals our otherwise obsessive concerns for a security that is, in fact, an illusion at best, a soul-shriveling poison at worst because it becomes a substitute god.

Death, the ultimate act of trust, gives the lie to all our imagined securities and shows them up for what they really are—hedges against life and life's challenges. Death is a constant reminder of the insecurity of life. But death is there to remind us only if we give it a space in our awareness.

Perspective on letting go is yet another gift our awareness of death has to give us. Watch how reluctantly and with such anguish, then temper, the two year old is made to let go of the ceramic (and breakable) vase she has picked up to explore. Therein we can see mirrored our lifelong reluctance to let go of what we clutch in our hands, in our hearts. Parents who are wise avoid the otherwise likely temper-tantrum by offering something else to substitute for what they're asking the child to let go of: a cookie, a favorite toy, something less breakable. One does not reason with a two year old.

Life is forever asking us to let go. To let go of the past. To let go of hatred and resentment. To let go of lost dreams (what might have been), lost loves. To let go of ruined and ruinous relationships. In every case, to let go of self-defeating, no-longer-working, destructive attachments. Our reluctance to let go, exactly like the two year old's, stems from having nothing (or thinking we have nothing) to take the place of what we're asked to let go of. The devil you know is better than the devil you don't. Letting go just for the sake of letting go doesn't make much sense. This is not the letting go that life, and therefore God and faith, asks of us.

If we are asked to let go, it is always for the possibility of something more, something better. If we see only the ending, the small death, and not the beginning, the new life, of course we are reluctant to let go. The problem is that interval of time between the ending (which is all we see and experience: the new beginning isn't in evidence yet) and what is to come next. Only hope and trust free us enough to endure the intervals between what was and what is coming to be. But isn't this why the Holy Spirit provides us with the gifts of hope and trust?

Death will demand that we let go of simply everything. Everything we've ever known and loved. Everyone. Our consciousness. Our very selves. But Jesus went on ahead of us through this total letting go into death and came back to show us that even here, that most of all here, this letting go of all that was is for something infinitely, unimaginably more. Only hope and trust can see us through the interval between the one and the other.

When we stop to think about it, is there anything that death is going to ask of us that a life of faith does not already ask? Life in so many ways asks us to relinquish our attempts to control in order that God's love may more and more be in control of our lives. Life challenges us to dismantle the walls we build for our security and to place our trust, not in our provident care but in God's. Life, over and over again, reaches out and bids us let go of what we are clutching to free our hands and our hearts to receive the better gift God offers us. A life of faith asks us to trust and hope, not merely in our own resources, but in God's infinite resourcefulness. What more than this will death, when it finally comes for us, ask? In God's compassionate and tender understanding of our slowness to learn, our fears, our fragile trust, God has given us all our lives to learn how to die. This is why it is good and holy to think about death, to give it a place in our awareness, to make friends with death.

For all that has been given to us, it has not been given us to know the details of our dying until that final event is upon us. Which, indeed, is not the least of God's mercies to us. When death will come. Precisely in what circumstances death will come. These we simply do not know. But these, after all, are mere details of the main event. There are, though, three far more important things we *can* know about our dying.

The first is this: as we live, so shall we die. Death is a part of the pattern of our lives, so interwoven into the texture of our lives it is of a piece with all the rest. Death does not stand apart from our living, a disconnected afterthought, a separate coda. The final note of the symphony is as much a part of the symphony as any of the other notes. A story's ending is as integral to it as its beginning and all that lies between the two. If we live a life of faith and trust, that's how we're going to die. If we live a life of giving ourselves freely, that's how we're going to die. If we let go peacefully when God asks this of us in life, that's how we're going to let go when God asks this of us in death. If we want to know how we're going to die, we need only look at how we live. If we are sincerely trying to live our lives in faith and hope and love, we have nothing to fear from our dying.

The second thing we can know about our dying is this: the Lord will be there with us. Jesus promised to be companion to us always, all the way home. The Lord who has been with us, faithfully, every step of our way will be there no less at our journey's end. The Lord who is there to grace us through all that life asks of us will be there when life makes its final demand. For many of us it is the thought of the sheer aloneness of our dying that we fear most. Our faith bids us set aside this fear. The one who died for us, who fed us the bread of life, who gave us his Holy Spirit, is faithful to his promises.

The third thing we can know about our dying is this: death is not the end for us, is not the end of us. Life as we know it here on earth is prologue and prelude to the fullness of life promised us in Jesus' resurrection. Death is merely the door we walk through to enter the room prepared for us in our Father's house. None of the euphemisms we concoct to deny death come close to its glorious reality: the end of life as we know it here, yes, but the beginning of an eternal fullness of life.

Here, finally, we meet head-on the linchpin of our Christian faith, without which all the rest is a tale for gullible fools, a cruel deception. The veracity of Jesus' revelations of who he was and who the Father is stands or falls with Jesus' resurrection. There is simply no room for hedging here; it is all-or-nothing. St. Paul put it this way: ". . . if Christ was not raised, your faith is worthless. . . . If our hopes in Christ are limited to this life only, we are the most pitiable of men" (1 Cor 15:17–19). For a Christian to see death without resurrection is the ultimate denial of Jesus Christ.

The resurrection, like the incarnation which began the story, is an event that defies the accumulated experience and wisdom of the human race from its beginning and down through all time. In every age, race, culture the one thing every human being has experienced is this: all living things die and death is the end of life. Anything else defies reason and the evidence of our senses. Who could possibly believe otherwise, in the face of all the evidence to the contrary, unless God had given us the living evidence of one exception? Magdalene at first thought he was the gardener. His apostles initially thought he was a ghost. Two disciples on their way to Emmaus at first thought he was a stranger who fell in with them along the road. Who can blame them? The truth was too preposterous. And yet it was true, as they came to see. And handed down to us to remember in every eucharist, to celebrate with joy every Easter. Our faith calls us to be an Easter people. When we see with the eyes of faith, nothing is only what it seems to be. Not even death.

Sorrow and pain are inescapably a part of our lives. We need not go looking to find these (though we may if we choose); they find us in and through all our vulnerabilities. They are life's small deaths. Joy and inner peace are not inescapably a part of our lives. They become a part of our lives only to the extent we choose to allow them. Which sounds strange indeed. Joy and inner peace a matter of our *choice*? If pain and sorrow are inevitably a part of our lives, why not joy and inner peace also? Besides, who in their right minds, given the choice, wouldn't choose joy and inner peace? The answer is: a truly astonishing number of people.

"I have set before you life and death, the blessing and the curse. Choose life, then, that you and your descendants may live, by loving the Lord, your God, heeding his voice, and holding fast to him. For that will mean life for you . . ." (Dt 30:19–20). The awesome truth is that we *do* have a choice between what is life-giving and what is deadening of the spirit. When all our excuses, rationalizations, evasions are stripped away, what is left is our *choosing* life or death. Not the least of our excuses is this one: but we don't know how!

When Thomas—he whose doubts so consistently mirror our own as to endear him to us forever—told Jesus that they did not know where Jesus was going and so didn't know how to get there, Jesus' response was this: "I am the way, and the truth, and the life" (Jn 14:6). Everything Jesus said, everything he did, showed us precisely how to choose life over death. And lest the details and the fine points be too much for us to grasp or remember, Jesus summed it all up for us: love God wholeheartedly, love others as you love yourself. The two, of course, are inseparable.

So it all comes down to this in the end, as it always does, no matter what path to it we follow: we either say yes to love and its imperatives or we say no; we either say yes to life, or we say no. Jesus clearly marked the only way to life, to joy and inner peace. There are no alternative routes. We can either take Jesus' word for it or try to find out for ourselves. He told us the kingdom of God is here and now in our midst, not all of it, but much more present, much more accessible to us than we think. It is possible for us to be far more peaceful and joyful than we could imagine. These are still ours for the asking.

All the vital signs of our faith are to be found in our love. St. Paul went so far as to say even a faith strong enough to move mountains is a dead faith without love (1 Cor 13:2). And where there are faith and love, there hope lives, completing the triune gifts of the Holy Spirit. No consideration of death and resurrection is complete without a word about hope.

Hope is the enduring sense, even in the midst of troubles, that it is all going to turn out all right, that God's loving word is going to have the final say. (Not to be confused with wishful thinking whereby we try to convince ourselves that everything is going to turn out the way we wish it.) Hope is the cornerstone of inner peace. Christian hope is simply a matter of taking Jesus at his word, in trusting that he lives up to his word and keeps his promises. Not a sparrow falls without the Father's consent. Not a tear is shed unheeded by God. God is that father avidly scanning the horizon for signs of the return home of his wandering son. God is the shepherd who leaves the ninety-nine sheep who are safe to seek out the lost and endangered lamb. God is . . . God is . . . God is love.

Christian hope is based on who God enduringly, un-changeably is.

Jesus didn't promise that our path would always be smooth, but he did promise to walk beside us to the end of the road. We need never be alone or abandoned. He didn't promise that our lives would be without pain and struggle, but he did promise that he would bring new life and growth out of our pain. As water wears a channel in the resisting earth so that it can flow, pain, if we let it, can hollow out a path through our resisting egotism so that compassion can flow through us. He didn't promise that he would take care of everything regardless of what we do, but he did promise to be willing partner in all our en-deavors, if we permit it. All we have to do is keep our half of the bargain.

Hope, as was said, is simply a matter of taking Jesus at his word.

These reflections began with death. Perhaps that is where they should also end.

Those of us fortunate enough to afford it often choose travel as part of our vacations. Travel can be a wonderful experience. Getting away for a while from the everyday parameters and cares of our life and work and looking at them from the outside. Seeing new and different places, new and different people, thinking different thoughts. Discovering how much larger the world is than the small part of it we inhabit. But is this not also true of every such trip? Though we might not have thought it possible when we set out with such excitement and eagerness to be away, a moment comes when we know: it's time to go home. And isn't this also true? We return home with a renewed appreciation of all that awaits us there with easy familiarity and promise.

Life's journey is no different. The moment comes when it is given us to know: it's time to go home. When that time comes God asks us to turn from what we are leaving behind and face what we are going to, whom we are going to: a God waiting to greet us with open arms and welcome us home. How do we know? Jesus went on ahead and came back to tell us and show us the way there.

Crucifixion

Has it not been ever so?
Love's first, eager partner joy.
But joy, that laughing, dancing
Siren of sunlit day
Goes not into night.

Love's nighttime partner pain.
Companion in the silent dark.
Hand-held where no other light
Bestows a kinder touch.
Love's final partner pain.

Shown us on a hill long ago.
Told us in wounded hands and feet
And dying heart.

Has it not been ever so?

But then comes the morning's dawn.

9. Making Friends with God-in-Me

*"The Lord called me from birth, from my
mother's womb he gave me my name" (Is 49:1).*

Every chapter in this book has considered some of the
ways God is present to the real and ordinary stuff of our
human experience, as it is here and now in our lives, not
as it might have been or could have been. We have considered some of the ways our faith might speak to and illu-
mine our human experience in the areas covered by each
chapter. Like a recurring melody in a symphony, a theme
running throughout, sometimes explicit and sometimes
not, is the indwelling of God's Holy Spirit within each of
us. Without this abiding presence within each of us nothing that has been said could really make sense. We are
asked to remember, as we look within, as we see and try to
understand what we find there, that we are treading on
holy ground, that we are moving in the precincts of God's
holy temple. We are asked to tread softly and with rever-
ent breath. And why? Only this: here is where God's Holy
Spirit dwells. Incredibly. (Our demons whisper to us:
Would *you* want *you* for a friend?) Shockingly. (Our
demons whisper to us: What is a nice person like God
doing in a place like *this?*) Absurdly. (Our demons whisper to us: Do you honestly believe that with literally everywhere to choose from, God would choose here?) And, yes,
mysteriously. Because most of the time we have no idea of
what God is up to within us.

In many ways a more distant God must seem more
comfortable. Why else do we try so to distance ourselves
from God? In many ways a God who paid not quite so

much attention to us must seem easier to deal with. Why else do we pay so little attention to God, as if hoping God won't notice us if we aren't looking? In many ways a God who didn't care so very much about us must seem less demanding. Why else do we think up all the reasons why God should care less about us? (Except, of course, when we are in trouble and need God's help.) There has to be *some* reason why we so effectively blunt our realization of God's unconditional love for us, why we are so surprised to hear it, so unable fully to believe it, much less to *experience* it.

It isn't as if God had made a secret of it, as if God were too reticent to tell us about it. It isn't as if Jesus were not clear enough on this point, had held back, skirted the issue, changed the subject. It isn't as if God hadn't shown us, did everything possible for us, showered us with gifts, until there was nothing left to give us but God's only Son. What more could God possibly have done for us, given to us? What more could Jesus have done for us? "There is no greater love than this: to lay down one's life for one's friends" (Jn 15:13). And as if even this were not enough, even in leaving us Jesus promised to send his Holy Spirit to be with us all the time, so we need never be alone. How has God failed us? In what way has God denied us?

Paul, like the other saints, allowed God's healing grace to open his eyes and his ears and his heart. He *heard* God's message of love that Jesus preached. And because he did he could make this amazing profession of faith: "Who will separate us from the love of Christ? Trial, or distress, or persecution, or hunger, or nakedness, or danger, or the sword? . . . I am certain that neither death nor life, neither angels nor principalities, neither the present nor the future, nor powers, neither height nor depth nor any other creature, will be able to separate us from the love of God that comes in Christ Jesus, our Lord" (Rom 8:5–39). Hardly a diffident statement. Which of us would dare to make such a statement and believe it?

When we stop to think about it, is this not a puzzling question? We who are so hungry to be loved, who seek it so avidly, so recklessly; we whose hearts light up at a smile of approval, a friendly hug, a word of recognition. Why on earth are we so determined *not* to believe that God truly *loves* us? What prevents us so effectively from feeling this in our hearts, experiencing it in our lives? What more could we want than God's own love and approval?

Whatever the reason, we have managed to keep God's love for us (exceedingly more reckless than ours) one of the best-kept secrets going, at least from ourselves. God's anger and displeasure with us, yes, God's disdain, disapproval, disappointment, even disgust with us—these we are all too prone to believe. But that God could cherish us, take delight in us, *like* us? This falls helplessly before the blockade we have so effectively erected. This falls on strangely deaf ears.

Perhaps, though, not so strangely if we do this, and do it honestly. Make a list of the feelings and attitudes we harbor toward ourselves. Then make a list of the feelings and attitudes that we are convinced God has toward us. Does not the curious match between the lists suggest what our blockade is constructed of, what has deafened our ears to this particular message? We simply assume, because we feel about ourselves the way we do, that this is how God must feel about us. We assume that our negative judgments of ourselves mirror God's judgments of us.

We may learn to hide this and disguise it (both our judgments of ourselves and God's putative judgments of us); most of us do so quite effectively. We learn so quickly what pleases others; with uncanny insight we divine what others want to hear, what others expect of us, what brings a smile, a clap on the back, a hug, a frown. (No polling service yet invented, with all the sophisticated and dazzling wizardry of computer science, can come close to assessing with such unerring accuracy as we can the reactions of others to *us*.) So we learn to wear a public face considerably different from the face that gazes back at us in the morning mirror over the sink.

But always, no matter how successful and charming our public disguise, in our heart of hearts we live with own real feelings for and judgments of ourselves. They speak to us whenever we receive a compliment or a word of praise or admiration, and they say within: if they only knew me as I *really* am. They speak to us in the silent spaces of the night, telling us how worthless, how lacking we are. They speak to us when we least expect it ("What do *you* know?" "Whom are you kidding?" "Who do you think you are?"), these treacherous inner voices that try to tell us who we are. These voices speak from the dark and secret places within us. In fact they require darkness and secrecy if they are to maintain their tyranny over us. As long as they are left in the dark, unshared, they can go uncontested by others who see in us things we can't see in ourselves, unchallenged by the evidence of truths at variance with their insidious message, even beyond the efficacious reach of God's loving revelation of who we are. These nay-saying inner voices are the barrier against which God's words crash, unheeded. These same voices, as long as they are kept hidden and unshared, have much to do with the sense of alienation and apartness that lurks around the edges of our every experience of companionship, even love. These voices not only insert a distance between ourselves and others, they distance us from our inner selves. No wonder they distance us from God and drown out the silent voice of the Holy Spirit within us.

The image of ourselves, howsoever inarticulate, we have formed is the mirror-image we have of what God thinks about us, how God feels about us. Moreover, our self-image greatly affects our image of who God is. The two are so intertwined that there is no pulling them apart, no having one without the other. If we are to hear and believe and—most important of all—*experience* what God has been trying to tell us about who we are, who God is, we have to find ways to remove the barriers, to still the nay-saying voices. There are several ways we can set the process in motion, if we want to; there are things we can do for ourselves. They are worth our attention.

Life, with or without our consent, imposes roles on every one of us, starting with male and female. Then family roles: father, mother, son, daughter, brother, sister, oldest, youngest. Outside-of-family roles: student, butcher, baker, candlestick maker; lover, friend, acquaintance, enemy. There are the roles that age imposes on us (as in, "Act your age!"): child, teenager, young adult, and so forth down the line. (We do seem to be getting more and more categories and sub-categories, don't we?) Then there are the roles we impose on ourselves: hero, villain, long-suffering martyr, ditto victim, rescuer, people pleaser, people displeaser. None of which comes close to exhausting the list of roles we deal with. Each role has its own set of rules, its own responsibilities, its own expectations and norms of success. Not infrequently these conflict with one another. No less infrequently, their sum total adds up to the impossible, give or take a few next-to-impossibles.

Naturally enough, we tend to identify ourselves with and by our roles. I am woman/man. I am a mother of three. I am a middle child. I am (God help me!) a teenager. I am a physician. I am _____. We each can fill in all these blanks. And, naturally enough, given our critical faculties, we tend to rank our performance in each of our various roles, giving birth to all the predicate adjectives, adjustable to each role, but they reduce to judgments of ourselves, regardless of role. I am good/bad. I am strong/weak, smart/dumb, all right/lousy and so forth. For most of us, "excellent," "very good," "superb," "unique" are adjectives we have no need of (even when others, in fact, do use them of us). Buried underneath the debris of all of this is the plain, unadorned inner self who is somehow involved in all these roles. When we make room in our conscious awareness for *this* self, which is neither defined nor contained by any of our roles, we are taking a giant step in the right direction.

As in everything else, God graciously showed us the way. Recall God's self-bestowed name revealed to Moses: I AM. Made in God's image, this is the truest name we can give ourselves: I am. To experience ourselves, all roles aside, as simply "I am" is to come closest to our authentic, God-given self-identity. Most of us have had these experiences, though we probably didn't recognize them as such.

For those of us fortunate enough to have experienced the grandeur and wonder of unspoiled nature, the I-am experience is the major ingredient (though mostly unrecognized, so un-self-conscious is the experience) of the exhilaration, sense of release, transporting-out-of-ourselves, at-one-with-all-that-is, even wholeness we experience there. Here, in this moment, it makes as much sense to say "I am tree!" or "I am mountain!" as it does to say "I am a thirty-five year old, married public accountant with two and a half children." Somehow, the former seems temporarily more true than the latter. That's because the I-am experience is at the heart of it. Similar moments occur in genuine human intimacy, in our experience of music, drama, play—about all of which we say, "They take me out of myself." The truth is the exact opposite: because these take us out of our roles they take us *into* that self which goes by no other name than I am. The self hidden under all that debris.

Silence and solitude, as we have considered, are indispensable for learning to become familiar with our inner selves. If we have the courage to give these a place in our lives, despite our fear of them, we can coax our inner selves into our conscious awareness, the single most important consciousness-raising we are capable of. As in any initial encounters between strangers, we can expect these encounters with our inner selves to be awkward at first, tongue-tied. But here is one place where there is no real need for words; in fact words are more likely to get in the way of the silent communion happening within. An encounter with our inner selves is much more a matter of an event we allow to happen than something we have to *make* happen. Let two compatible people get together and nature takes care of the rest. The trick is getting them together. Finding ways to get together with our inner selves is half the battle.

Another way we can help in the process of encountering our inner selves is held out to us by others. Rather than brushing aside and dismissing out of hand compliments, words of appreciation and praise (the airy, "Oh that was nothing"), we can take time to reflect on them. Of course there are compliments that are more flattery than sincerely meant, but these carry their own identifying marks. There are also compliments that come from the heart, small acts of honesty and courage on the part of others who speak the truth as they see it. They are neither liars nor flatterers. More often than we think, though our inner selves may be hidden from us, they are not so hidden from others who can see in us what we can't yet see in ourselves. We do well to take their compliments seriously.

Another way we can help our inner selves emerge into the light of God's love is learning to *forgive* ourselves. We can become so obsessively, so fearfully preoccupied with trying to persuade, cajole, con God into forgiving us, we are simply blind to the fact that we do not forgive ourselves. God does not need to be talked into forgiving us. All those carefully rehearsed arguments the prodigal son concocted and played over in his head as he made his way home, arguments as to why his father should allow him back, at least as a servant, evaporated into thin air as needless in the overwhelming love of his father's welcome. God is infinitely more ready to forgive us than we are to let God's forgiveness into our hearts. The problem lies with our willingness to forgive ourselves.

What, though, does it mean to forgive ourselves? Perhaps seeing what it means to forgive someone else will shed some light. When we perceive ourselves to be sinned against, wronged, offended by someone, our initial reaction is hurt, closely followed by anger, resentment, and the desire to punish, to strike back and hurt as we have been hurt. We experience a fracture in the oneness, the harmony of the relationship (anything from hairline to a major break, depending on the gravity of the wrong). We experience an alienation from the one who has sinned against us. As long as our sinned-against-feelings prevail and have their say, we look for ways to punish the offending party, to get even, as a way of assuaging these feelings. This process feeds insidiously off itself. Thus even a hairline fracture can widen, a more serious break become close to impossible to mend. In the meanwhile, the original offending party now becomes offended by being punished, setting in motion a reciprocal process of anger and punishment. All the ingredients of all-out warfare between two people. Allowed to escalate uninterrupted, the process leads to complete alienation, the breaking off of all relations.

Forgiveness short-circuits this process. Not that we feel no hurt, anger, desire to punish, or have no need to give legitimate expression to these feelings. But having expressed them, we do not proceed to act them out by punishing the one who offended us. We see that punishing the other is not the way to assuage these feelings; forgiveness is. So we forgive, we waive any right to exact retribution (as God does with us). Forgiveness effects reconciliation, heals alienation. Often the reconciliation brings about a closer, more understanding relationship than existed before the disruption.

When we perceive ourselves (rightly or wrongly, it makes no difference) to be sinned against by ourselves, exactly the same process is set in motion. The desire to hurt, to punish, is no less a part of this process, even though it is ourselves that we hurt and punish. The same alienation, the same disruption of harmony, is no less a part of this process. We are alienated from ourselves; our inner harmony is fractured. Unless we forgive ourselves, self-punishing processes continue (guilt, depression, added fuel for the nay-saying voices within), the sense of alienation from our selves increases. Refusal to forgive ourselves is a barrier that effectively blocks the healing power of God's forgiveness of us. Without self-forgiveness the question of whether or not God forgives us is largely academic, for all the difference it makes to us.

Even when we do learn, with God's grace, to begin forgiving ourselves so that we do not live with self-hatred and self-alienation, lack of wholehearted forgiveness can remain. To the extent that it does, we find it far easier to be compassionate, understanding, forgiving of others than we do of ourselves. We can treat others with a kindness and gentle consideration that is notably lacking in our treatment of ourselves. This merely indicates that our self-forgiveness isn't yet complete.

The process of coming to know our inner selves is not something we have to do alone, without the help of anyone else. Others can be of enormous help, if we permit them. Not everyone, of course, but those who, by their no-strings-attached acceptance of us as we are, give us permission to be ourselves with them. With the help of such as these we can find the courage to share our experience of ourselves as it really is, nay-saying voices and all. We can give external voice to these hidden, secret voices, bring them out in the open where we can see them for what they are—bullying liars, deniers and distorters of our truth. Like all bullies, they back down when we confront them; like all liars, they can't stand to be exposed to the light of the truth. We can give external voice also to our fears, our aspirations, our unanswered questions, our real failings, the way we really think. The reason this can be so healing is not primarily that another sees us as we are, but that *we* come to see ourselves more clearly in the process of telling ourselves to someone else.

In this we can truly be healers for one another, the instruments of God's grace. When we love one another as God loves us, we can work what is probably the greatest miracle of healing: by allowing one another to be, we loosen the shackles that imprison our inner selves. No wonder, next to loving God, this is the greatest of the commandments! That we be for one another what God is for us. We can be this for one another, though, only if we let God's love for us live in our hearts. It is the power of God's love in us, not merely our own limited capacity to love, which works the miracle.

The brush that yields to and does not resist the strokes of the artist is participant in the work of art. The work of art is the artist's: there are no brushes immortalized in the history of art. The work of art expresses the artist, not the brush. Nonetheless, there could be no work of art without the instrumentality of the brush. In the divine plan of our salvation—a plan, be it noted, devised in God's wisdom, not ours—we are the instruments of God's saving grace, each one of us. Life is not a spectator sport. Nor is salvation. Much as we might like at times to opt out, to bid everyone else to go on ahead without us, this is choosing death, not life. We are not interchangeable objects, one serving as well, if not better, than another. If we opt out, there is no one to take our place. If we opt out, there is a song that will never be sung, a story that will never be told. Much as the nay-saying voices within might tell us we are worthless, we are good for nothing, they are liars. And no amount of repetition ever changed a lie into the truth.

Jesus left us a common-sense, down-to-earth criterion for figuring out what something is really all about: by their fruits you shall know them. "Beware of false prophets who come to you disguised as sheep but underneath are ravenous wolves. You will be able to tell them by their fruits. Can people pick grapes from thorns, or figs from thistles? In the same way, a sound tree produces good fruit but a rotten tree bad fruit. A sound tree cannot bear bad fruit, nor a rotten tree bear good fruit. Any tree that does not produce good fruit is cut down and thrown on the fire. I repeat, you will be able to tell them by their fruit" (Mt 7:16–20).

False prophets, that's what these inner nay-saying voices ultimately are, and what they are all about. We may disguise them as humility, as honest self-knowledge, as the brutal truth. But their fruits betray the disguise: these voices counsel irresponsibility, they provide the excuse, the alibi for not taking responsibility for the goodness in us. This is their under-the-table pay-off. If one has nothing worthwhile to give, one is thereby exempt from giving. If one is not good enough, one can hardly be held to blame for not attempting the impossible. If one is nothing, then nothing is all that can be reasonably expected. These voices counsel death, not life; they are the true voices of suicide in all its forms. No one, after all, can be blamed for throwing away what is worthless.

To admit into our conscious awareness God's unshakable love for us means accepting also our own response-ability. "I can't" is a lie; "I won't" is the truth. "It is more than I have to give" is a lie; we are never asked to give more than we have to give. "I am worthless" is a lie; in God's eyes each of us is worth the life and death of God's only Son. "No one loves me" is the greatest lie of all; even if no one else does, Father, Son, and Holy Spirit love us beyond anything we'd dare hope.

A basic willingness at least to be as honest with ourselves as we can be is the first step on the path to any healing. If we just can't be bothered, if we're too scared, too sinful, too uncertain, too busy, we are far better off admitting to ourselves at least this much of the truth.

This admission leaves the door of our self-imposed cell ajar, capable of being nudged wider open with God's grace, whereas each lie we tell ourselves slams the door shut—in God's face and in our own. But even when we do slam the door shut, our compassionate Lord never slams his door on us. He waits patiently outside ours, for the merest crack to let him get a foot in.

Paul prayed that we would not slam the door shut. "This, then, is what I pray, kneeling before the Father, from whom every family, whether spiritual or natural, takes its name: Out of his infinite glory, may he give you the power through his Spirit for your hidden self to grow strong, so that Christ may live in your hearts through faith, and then, planted in love and built on love, you will with all the saints have the strength to grasp the breadth and the length, the height and the depth, until, knowing the love of Christ, which is beyond all knowledge, you are filled with the utter fullness of God. Glory to him whose power, working within us, can do infinitely more than we can ask or imagine . . ." (Eph 3:14–21).

God wants nothing less for us than to fill our emptiness to the brim. But even God, so much does our maker think of us, waits on our permission, our willingness, our openness to receive. *We* set the limits on God's largesse.

How tragic that we fear God wants in only to take from us what we are loath to part with, to ask of us what we are not yet ready to give up. We fear what God might demand of us if we let God in, what stern, displeased, angry noises God is going to make at the sight of the mess and clutter, the sheer disorder of the inside of our house. (Better to wait until we've had the chance to straighten things up before entertaining the landlord.) All those long, dolorous faces of the saints in religious art come back to haunt us, daunt us: we have no desire to join their unhappy ranks, to join the anguish written on their faces. Perhaps one day we can arrange an at-home for God, but certainly not now, certainly not like this. Even if we work up our courage and invite God into the carefully straightened-up living room, we certainly don't want God roaming through the rest of the house at will. And so doors remained closed. And so God waits, like the father of that other prodigal.

We confuse giving with giving up, as if what we give were lost to us. So we fear giving ourselves lest we lose ourselves. We fear intimacy for the same reason. We are so unused to gifts that come no-strings-attached (other than those that hold the wrapping), we fear even to receive what others want to give us. The sinful ways we treat one another do not prepare us to believe or trust a God whose giving is utterly free, unearned, unearnable. We keep looking for the catch. There's *always* a catch. At least with us.

In spite of this, if we don't give ourselves at least the opportunity to practice trust with one another, to get the hang of the thing by *doing* it (i.e. trusting), if we don't risk taking a chance on one another, for all the bruises and aching heart muscles that entails, how else are we ever going to learn to trust God? If kindergarten is really more than we can handle, are we ready for the first grade? To paraphrase John (1 Jn 4:20), anyone who says, "I trust God," and does not trust brother or sister is a liar, since one who does not trust the brother or sister who can be seen cannot trust God who is not seen.

If there is any catch, it is this: God chose *us* to show the face of God's love to one another. We are God's vocabulary, living words to give voice to God's goodness in and through our goodness, to give voice to God's compassion, tenderness, caring, faithfulness in and through us. We have this on no less authority than that of the word of God, Jesus Christ. He said it and showed it in so many ways, only one of which was this one. After he washed the feet of his apostles at their final dinner together, he said this to them: "I have given you an example so that you may copy what I have done for you" (Jn 13:15). Copying Jesus. Faith in the word of God makes us words of God. With what kind of voice do we allow God to speak through us? Is the God we so often accuse of being silent actually rendered mute by us, God's living words?

Jesus told us what it was going to take for the world to believe that he was truly sent by the Father. So he prayed for us: "May they all be one. Father, may they be one in us, as you are in me and I am in you, so that the world may believe that it was you who sent me" (Jn 17:21). Jesus placed his credibility in our hands! His credibility in the world depends on us who call ourselves Christian; it depends on our oneness with each other, it depends on the way we love and trust one another. Which may be a very hard saying, but Jesus said it.

Perhaps there always *is* a catch, because here is another: we cannot be one with each other unless we are one with ourselves; each of us has to possess a *me* before we can be part of an *us*. Which brings us yet again to what this whole book has been about from the beginning: making friends with *me,* or, to say the same slightly differently, making friends with God-in-me. We cannot make friends with God unless we make friends with our inner selves. There it is. If there were another way, surely we with all our ingenuity would have found it by now. There simply isn't any other way.

Me. What a sign of contradiction! Byword in our common language for selfishness and self-preoccupation (as in "the me-generation" and "what's in it for me?"). Shorthand in our private inner language for the villain of the piece, the culprit, the fear-filled coward, the real cause of all our problems. The cell in which each of us is locked. And, at the same time, another *me* entirely. The one who brings a smile to another's face. The one who is capable of being tender and loving, compassionate. The one who yearns to be all there is to be, to give all there is to give, who hopes for the moon and dances under the stars. *Me.* All of this in a first-person singular pronoun!

Language again, and all the ways it misleads us, the grammar of it, the two-faced words of it. Here is yet another way. It seems easier to understand and talk about be-ing if we make nouns (or pronouns) out of what really are verbs, i.e. words designating *action.* "Reify" is the intimidating Latin-derived word for this process (*res,* thing; *facere,* to make: to make into a thing). Electricity is an example. Grammatically, a noun, a thing; in reality, an action. Thus have we done with *me. Me* is an ongoing action. Two other nouns-that-should-be-verbs might help rescue us from confusion at this point. These are river and story.

Combine in equal parts the nature of water, the nature of the earth's surface, and the influence of gravity; the interplay of these produces what we name a river. From the mountaintops mere rivulets pour down, joining up with streamlets, flow into streams, flow into the river. Water flowing—that's what a river is, water *river*-ing its way to the ocean. Is a river deep? Yes. Is a river shallow? Yes. Is a river wide and gentle? Yes. Is a river narrow and violent? Yes. Is a river pure or polluted? Yes. Life-giving or destructive? Yes. Cold or warm? Yes. Just like *me.*

Combine in equal parts human nature, the nature of life's course, and the influence of the Holy Spirit; the interplay of these produces what we name a *me. Me* is the name we give to the individual instance of human be-ing that is each of us. If there were such a verb it should probably be *me-ing.* We *me* our way over the course life sets before us, from our mountaintop beginnings to the ocean waiting to receive us when our *me-ing* has run its course. All the questions we ask about the river we can ask about the *me.* And they are answered in the same way. *Me* is no more static than a river is. *Me* can no more exist in isolation than a river can. Neither *me* nor river can be contained by nouns or adjectives. That's only the way we talk about them. The words are not to be confused with the realities they merely point to. Does the river end when it has emptied its waters into the ocean? If so, what about all those rivulets and streamlets, at that very same moment, flowing down the mountainsides? Nouns are easier to deal with than verbs.

Combine in equal parts a storyteller, someone to listen, and the influence of a muse; and the interplay of these produces what we name a story. Every story has a beginning and a middle and an ending. Things happen in stories. Are stories true or false? Yes. Are stories happy or sad? Yes. Long or short? Yes. Do stories really happen or not? Yes. Are stories really over when they're ended or not? Yes. Stories happen wherever there is a storyteller, wherever listeners gather.

Me is like the river. *Me* is like the story. Except, in this latter case, *me* is both the story and the teller.

Each of us has been given a story to tell. It is our story and we are the storyteller. An actor who plays in a drama is assigned a role chosen by someone else, in a story told by someone else, lines to say written by another, interactions with the other characters already determined by the playwright. This is not an apt metaphor for life. Our story is not told by someone else. We write our own lines. We are not the sole determinant of the interaction between and among the characters in our story, but we are solely responsible for our contribution to these interactions. The relative importance of each character in our story is assigned by us. Whether our story be a love story or a story of hatred and war, a success story or one of failure, a story concocted largely from dreams and imagination or a realistic story—all of this is up to us. We are *telling* the story. It is so easy for us to fall into the role of actor and forget the story is ours to tell. If we don't like the direction the story is moving in, we can change it. Should some of the characters interfere with our telling of the story, we can reassign their role in the story or write them out of the story.

As with every storyteller we have to rely on our sense of what *fits* the story, what is right for the story, given the kind of ending we have in mind. We have to decide fairly soon into the story the kind of ending we want for it, as artistic integrity demands that the whole story be of a piece with the ending, that the whole story builds up to and is realized in its ending. Every story of any length has chapters. A good storyteller recognizes when one chapter is finished and it's time to take the story to the next chapter. Most storytellers get better at it as they go along, as they get more into their story and develop greater empathy with their characters. Most good storytellers resist the temptation to go off on self-indulgent tangents that do nothing to carry the story forward or develop the characters, that contribute nothing to the story's ending. A good storyteller always keeps the listeners in mind. There is one thing that no storyteller can do: give over the telling of his story to someone else.

If the storyteller is blessed, there are those who want to hear the story. Every one of us, in our deepest hearts, wants to tell our story to others who will listen to it. No human tragedy is quite so heartbreaking as a storyteller with no one to listen. In the final analysis, what else do we really have to give each other than to listen and hear each other's stories, with respect and reverence? There are few more meaningful words we can say to each other than these: tell me your story and I will listen.

Our faith adds a dimension to this analogy that would not otherwise be there. In fact, each of us is *not* the sole teller of our story. God—the greatest storyteller of all—is the silent co-author of our stories. So it is both our story and God's story. God determines the final length of the story. God determines most of the circumstances in which the story is told. But apart from that, we share fairly equally authorship rights. For such a master story-teller, God is graciously, lovingly deferential in the partnership, even when the story takes directions that are not God's.

Even the ancients knew that every storyteller has to have a muse, a source of inspiration, a quiet voice within to guide the telling of the story. We have not been left without our muse. The Holy Spirit is there to inspire and guide the telling of our story, if we are willing to be listener as well as teller. While all our God-given talents are needed in the telling of our story, a munificent God makes available to us God's own boundless resources, there for the asking. But God is careful not to infringe on our author's rights in the partnership. God is there to help in the telling; but only if we want the help.

And when our story is finally done, the telling of it finished? Jesus has promised us this: God, the lover of stories and storytellers, will still be there. And God will say to us: "Tell me your story. I'd really like to hear it."

After all, it's God's story too.

And God will give us all the time in the world.

A Sinner's Prayer

Peter said it for us all, Lord,
"Depart from me . . ."
And yet You stay.
I'd have long since left
Anyone who treated me as shabbily
As I do You.

I wish I could see what You see
In me. What's there
That captivates You so.
What stays You here

At my side,
Ignored, forgotten.

But, Lord, even as I search in vain
For reasons to believe in me,
To trust my fragile possibilities,
Do You believe for both of us,
And trust for me
In me.